Prairie Gothic

Prairie Gothic:

The Story of a West Texas Family

John R. Erickson

Number Three in the Frances B. Vick Series

University of North Texas Press
Denton, Texas

The paper used in this book meets the minimum requirements of the
American National Standard for Permanence of Paper for Printed Library
Materials, z39.48.1984. Binding materials have been chosen for durability.

Library of Congress Cataloging-in-Publication Data

Erickson, John R., 1943-
 Prairie gothic : the story of a West Texas family / John R. Erickson ; foreword
by Elmer Kelton.
  p. cm. -- (Frances B. Vick series ; no. 3)
 Includes bibliographical references and index.
 ISBN-13: 978-1-57441-200-0 (cloth : alk. paper)
 ISBN-10: 1-57441-200-0 (cloth : alk. paper)
 ISBN-13: 978-1-57441-203-1 (pbk. : alk. paper)
 ISBN-10: 1-57441-203-5 (pbk. : alk. paper)
 1. Erickson, John R., 1943---Family. 2. Erickson, John R., 1943---Homes
and haunts--Texas, West. 3. Novelists, American--20th century--Family
relationships. 4. Novelists, American--20th century--Biography. 5. Texas,
West--Social life and customs. 6. Rural families--Texas, West. 7. Texas, West-
-Biography. I. Title. II. Series.

PS3555.R428Z47 2005
813'.54--dc22

                                                              2005016189

Prairie Gothic is Number Three in the Frances B. Vick Series

This book is dedicated to my mother,
Anna Beth Curry Erickson

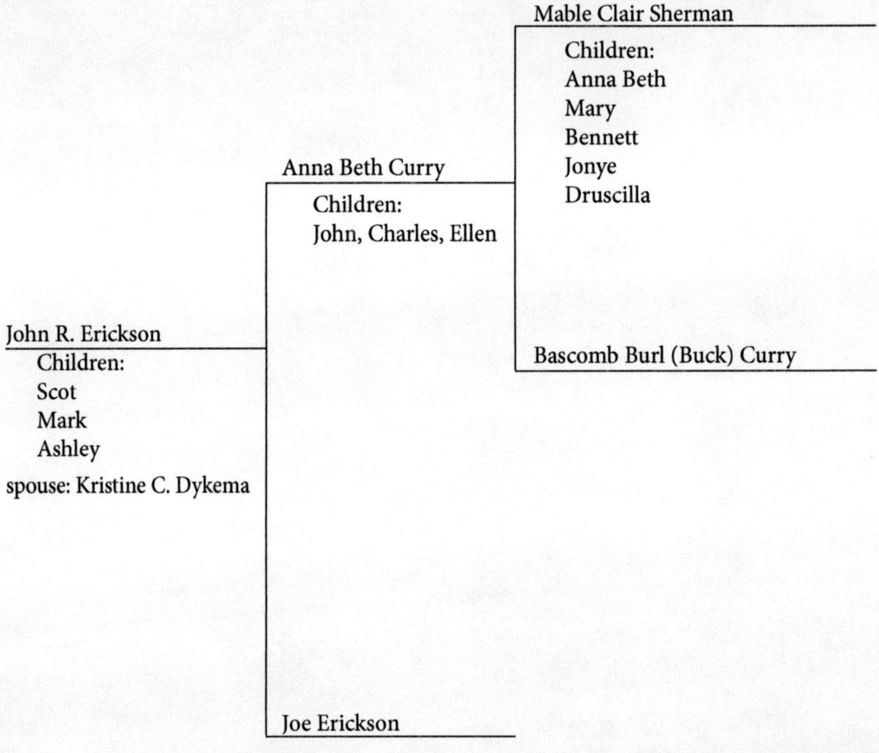

Mable Clair Sherman

Children:
Anna Beth
Mary
Bennett
Jonye
Druscilla

Anna Beth Curry

Children:
John, Charles, Ellen

John R. Erickson
Children:
Scot
Mark
Ashley

spouse: Kristine C. Dykema

Bascomb Burl (Buck) Curry

Joe Erickson

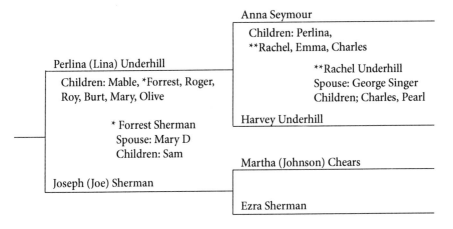

Anna Seymour

Children: Perlina,
**Rachel, Emma, Charles

Perlina (Lina) Underhill

                        **Rachel Underhill
Children: Mable, *Forrest, Roger,   Spouse: George Singer
Roy, Burt, Mary, Olive   Children; Charles, Pearl

           * Forrest Sherman   Harvey Underhill
           Spouse: Mary D
           Children: Sam   Martha (Johnson) Chears

Joseph (Joe) Sherman

                         Ezra Sherman

Sarah Elizabeth Bennett

John A. Curry

"The great outdoors does something for people. The prairie and sky had a way of trimming people down to size or changing them into giants—into people to whom nothing seemed impossible. I think you should learn something about your cowboy ancestors. You have a little of their blood in you—and it is good blood."

Mary D Sherman, rancher's wife, writing to her grandchildren

"Regionalism and provincialism are not the same thing. To be a Texan is to be the heir of distinguished cultural and historical traditions that breed dignity and gentility in Texans who will learn and understand."

Frederick W. Rathjen, Historian (Rathjen 1998: xi)

"Professional history tends to regard a fascination with place as antiquarian. But mythology is all about place. . . . Mythology makes ordinary places the scenes of great events, thus giving them extraordinary power."

Dan Flores, Author (Flores 1990: 48)

Contents

Foreword

Given an assignment to compose an essay in a long-ago English course at the University of Texas, I wrote a piece about ranch life in West Texas. The teacher approved of my writing but deplored my subject matter.

"You will never become a writer unless you choose subjects of importance," she told me.

In her view I had committed the literary sin of provincialism. She did not see that life everywhere is important, that all human experience has value whether in an urban environment like New York, Paris or Rome, or in some isolated hamlet, ranch, or farm miles from the interstate. At some level, the human condition is universal.

John Erickson discovered this truth as he gradually became aware of his own forebears and their roles in a history only sketchily recorded and but dimly remembered. He came, over time, to appreciate the significance of the dusty, formidable plains where they lived out their lives fighting loneliness, drought, and a hundred other obstacles. History is much more than just the recounting of selected extraordinary events and extraordinary people. It is or should be the accumulated experience of common people who rarely if ever saw their names in print, who met the everyday challenges of life the best they could and either survived or succumbed to them. Often they were swept along by conditions and events over which they had little control. They endured hardships we can only imagine, and occasionally saw violence of the rawest kind.

Erickson's great-great grandmother, Martha Sherman, was murdered by Comanche raiders. His great-grandfather, Joe Sherman, died of a bullet wound inflicted by a quarrelsome neighbor. If these people's stories did not make it into the officially accepted historical records, they nevertheless deserve to be remembered. We are all products of our forebears, the long generations that came before us. We must understand them if we are to understand ourselves. They are part of who we are, what we are, and where we are.

Erickson points out in this remembrance of his ancestors that they were not always as upright, brave, and tolerant as we might wish them to have been, but they were human. They had strengths we can admire, and they had weaknesses we can understand because we share those weaknesses.

We are fortunate that he has recorded this clear-eyed but affectionate recounting of these pioneer families, for thousands of similar family sagas have disappeared with little to show for them except names carved on weathering tombstones. They are forever gone because no one saw the importance of preserving them. Future generations are the poorer for their loss.

Building on stories heard from his mother when he was a boy, Erickson spent years interviewing family members and digging through musty old records, piecing the family story together like a jigsaw puzzle. The picture that slowly came into focus was unique to his own people, yet in many ways universal. His forebears won their victories and suffered their defeats, had their periods of happiness and their times of tragedy, like almost any family anywhere. In reading about them we can hear echoes of our own kin. We can relate to the internal forces that drove them and the demons that sometimes bedeviled them. Many of those forces, and many of those demons, are still with us.

Erickson's forebears crossed trails with several historic figures such as the family of the tragic Comanche captive, Cynthia Ann Parker; Oliver Loving, mortally wounded by Indians in New Mexico and brought back by Charles Goodnight for burial at home in Texas; Tom

Ross, the notorious outlaw, instigator of a double murder in Seminole, Texas. Erickson skillfully interweaves the past and the present and often quotes differing viewpoints about people and events to show us all sides. He makes us feel the emotions of the many characters he brings to life. Some are happy, some sad, some simply frustrated, but all are engaging.

He describes wonderful moments of epiphany. There is, for example, his unexpected discovery of his cowboy grandfather's sizeable library, accumulated over many years by a man who had but four years of formal schooling, yet educated himself by voracious and selective reading. In that library Erickson found an account of his great-great-grandmother's murder, written by historian J. Evetts Haley, Goodnight's biographer. Erickson describes his nervousness at first meeting the stern and conservative Haley, a man who saw value in the history of one's own family and one's own surroundings, however insignificant they might appear to others.

That is the spirit in which John Erickson approached this work. In a sense, the story of his ancestors reflects the stories of all our ancestors, for we can see parallels to accounts we have heard about our own. In his mirror we can see our own reflections.

Elmer Kelton

Preface

This is a book I tried to write many times over the years, but somehow it kept eluding me. In my first attempts I approached it as a piece of impersonal history, where I hovered above the story and simply directed traffic. When that didn't bring a good result (too stiff, no passion), I tried stepping into the story and giving myself a strong voice. That failed too, this time because the writing became too emotional.

Then I tried several times to make it a novel, but that yielded the worst results of all. Released from the discipline of history, I made the characters whomever I wanted them to be, and that was wrong. So I put my research notes away in a drawer and forgot about them. Years passed, decades. When I went back to the material in May of 2004, my motivation was simple and thoroughly unprofessional: I needed an escape from the boredom of sitting in my writing office every morning for five hours. Anything would do.

This volume began without fanfare, cunning, or literary ambition, and it felt right from the start. The first draft came quickly and I finished it in six weeks, although revisions and additional research kept me busy for several more months. This brings to mind a nugget of psychology gleaned from four decades of matching wits with horses. When you desperately need one for some pasture work, if the horse senses your need, he will laugh at your offer of sweet feed and leave you afoot. The best way to catch a clever horse is to convince him, through an elaborate theatrical performance, that you really don't care whether he comes into feed or not. So it was with the writing of this story. When I gave up stalking the beast, it plodded into the corral, and I managed to slip around and shut the gate.

The voice I have used is a combination of storyteller and historian, and the result might be something close to what Dan Flores has called mythic history: the record of a people in the context of a specific place that has shaped them. That place is the flatland prairie of northwestern Texas that has gone by various names (High Plains, South Plains, Staked Plains, and Llano Estacado), as well as the rugged country on its eastern boundary, often referred to as the "caprock canyonlands."

I am better suited to storytelling than to scholarly pursuits, but I recognize the importance of a disciplined treatment of the past. It really *does* matter when and where an event occurred, and who said so, and I have tried to adhere to the high standards of historical research laid down by the scholars in my region who have blazed a clear trail: J. Evetts Haley, W. C. Holden, David Murrah, Dan Flores, Charles Townsend, Frederick Rathjen, Jack T. Hughes, John Cooper Jenkins, Ernest Wallace, E. A. Hoebel, and Pauline and R. L. Robertson.

My scholarship isn't likely to impress professional historians, but they might recognize it as a pretty good effort for a purveyor of dog stories.

In documenting my sources, I have adopted the system used by archeologists. It seems the simplest and least intrusive of any I have found. It takes the form (Rathjen 1973: 44), listing the author, year of publication, and page number. Readers who wish to check a reference can turn to the References for the complete citation. Unless the source is cited as a letter, interview, magazine, or newspaper article, it came from a book. This system suits me, and I hope that readers will approve.

Finally, I need to pass out flowers to the many people who have helped me in my research:

To my mother, grandmother, and great-uncles, all deceased, who were kind and patient enough to answer my questions in interviews and letters. They are mentioned in the text and bibliography, and the importance of their contributions should be clear enough. Without them, there would be no stories to tell.

To my Aunt Bennett Kerr, always a reliable source of family lore; cousin Mike Harter who offered advice and criticism of the manuscript, and drew the maps; and cousins Barbara Whitton and Martha Marmaduke who gave encouragement and spent many hours gathering up family photographs.

To the archivists and librarians at the Southwest Collection, Texas Tech University, Lubbock; the Panhandle-Plains Historical Museum in Canyon; the Crosby County Pioneer Museum in Crosbyton; the Southwestern Writers Collection at Texas State University; the Nita Stewart Haley Library in Midland; the Texas Archives in Austin; the Barker Library at the University of Texas; The Microfilm Center in Dallas; Martin County Historical Museum and the Martin County Convent Foundation in Stanton; and the Perry Memorial Library in Perryton; also Amy Bearden and Jody Logsdon.

And finally, to Kris, my wife, friend, and helpmate of thirty-seven years.

Chapter One: Anna Beth

It was my great fortune to have been raised by a woman who loved language, told wonderful stories, and believed that passing those stories along to me was more important than doing other things for herself. That was my mother, Anna Beth Curry Erickson. I was the last of three children and by the time I came along and reached the age of five, Mother had time to spend with me. We went everywhere together and became the best of friends. I spent many hours sitting on a stool in the kitchen, watching her wash the dishes and prepare meals, and in the afternoons we snuggled up in her bed for Bible stories and a nap. We raised ducks, rabbits, and chickens in the back yard, and from her I learned to wring a chicken's neck and pluck the feathers after dipping the bird into boiling water, skills she had learned from her mother and grandmother. We raised a garden, collected horned toads, and hung out the weekly wash on the clothesline.

Wherever we were, she told me stories about her family in West Texas. Some involved kinfolks I had met: my Sherman great-uncles, Roy, Burt, and Roger; their sisters, Aunt Olive and Grandmother Curry; Great-grandmother Perlina Sherman; and Buck Curry, my grandfather. Other stories involved people more distant, whose faces I had to create in my imagination: the Quaker Underhills; Martha Sherman, who died under a Comanche scalping knife; Tom Ross, the notorious outlaw and killer; and my great-grandfather, Joe Sherman, always a figure of great mystery.

Author's mother and father, Joe and Anna Beth Erickson, and author's brother Charles. 1939.

Mother's stories had the quality of myth, grand stories that weren't tied to a specific time or place, and in my young imagination, these people occupied the same legendary space that included my favorite characters from the Old Testament: David the Shepherd Boy, Moses, Daniel, Joseph, and Samuel. Until years later when I began tracking down some of the family stories in books and archives, I was never sure those people actually lived and did the things my mother described.

I discovered not only that they were real people, but that through some mysterious alchemy, I had become part of their drama. I remember exactly the day in 1968 when this revelation came to me. I was in my second year of studies at Harvard Divinity School, walking through the snow in the Yard near Widner Library. Suddenly I stopped and looked around and it hit me like a thunderbolt: "I will never be part of this." I was wearing the correct clothes, had shed my Texas accent, and had acquired the patina of a cosmopolitan man, but it was false.

Three months later, I left Cambridge, three hours short of a master's degree in theology, moved back to Texas, and began the long process of burrowing deep into my roots. It took me to cowboy jobs in the Texas and Oklahoma Panhandles, into small town libraries and newspaper offices and the homes of ranchers and cowboys; to weddings and funerals and family reunions; back to West Texas and the land that had been the setting for Mother's stories. I didn't have a name for what I was doing, but I know now that I was looking for stories and a voice for telling them. When I finally found that voice around 1981, it bore a striking resemblance to Anna Beth's. She never heard of *Hank the Cowdog*, but had she lived to read those tales, she would have recognized her voice and earthy sense of humor on every page.

This is the story of her family in West Texas, the Underhills, Singers, Shermans, and Currys. Anna Beth is not one of the characters. In a fashion typical of her whole approach to life, she left herself out of most of the stories, choosing instead to focus on people she considered more important. And yet, in spite of herself, she becomes the main character—veiled, perhaps, but present on almost every page. She was the one who remembered, shaped, and told the stories, and made them so vivid in my imagination that I never forgot them.

Anna Beth Curry at her father's ranch in Gaines County, with cowboy Lane Barton. 1935.

Chapter Two: The Visit

During the summer of 1966 I was in Austin, finishing up a few courses at the University of Texas so that I could graduate in August, and my thoughts had turned eastward. I had been accepted as a student at Harvard Divinity School and soon I would be moving to Cambridge, leaving Texas behind, perhaps forever. The thought of spending some time in Cambridge excited me. During the Kennedy administration, we had heard a great deal about Harvard University. President Kennedy, his brother Bobby, Defense Secretary McNamara, and other members of the administration had studied there. Could a kid from Perryton compete with the luminous beings who occupied such a place? I wasn't sure, but I had a ticket for finding out.

So why, in the midst of such heady speculations, did I write my grandmother in Seminole and ask if I could spend a weekend with her? Apparently four years of university education had failed to do what I had hoped it would do, erase all memory of my background in rural West Texas. I had wanted to vault into a more important world that didn't include cowboys, cotton gins, grain elevators, or tumbleweeds, but by the summer of 1966 I had begun to feel a stirring of curiosity about my forebears. The stories I had grown up with had begun to murmur in the back of my mind.

In my youth, Grandmother Curry had seemed a kind but rather distant figure, stern and dignified. She had raised five daughters and buried one husband, and now she occupied the old Curry house in an orderly solitude that seemed to suit her very well. When I was young, even my mother felt some uneasiness about visiting her, as our visits brought the shouts of grandchildren and the constant threat of broken lamps and vases. Grandmother never made us feel unwelcome, but Mother always suspected that she heaved a sigh of relief when she saw us backing out of her driveway, waving goodbye.

I typed my letter on good stationery and took special care to make it neat and proper. I had exchanged enough letters with Grandmother to know that she wrote near-flawless English and would think less of me if my letter revealed a lower standard. The irony of this didn't occur to me until years later: that I, a senior at the University of Texas, feared the scrutiny of a woman who gotten an eighth grade education in the one-room school for ranch children. Grandmother's reply came a week later, saying that she would be delighted for me to visit and that she had instructed Mrs. Tinnell, her housekeeper, to make a special trip to the Piggly Wiggly to stock up on groceries, especially beef. She ended by saying that my great-uncle Roy Sherman had reported that the grass at the ranch needed a rain. This hardly came as a surprise. The grass in Gaines County, Texas, always needed a rain.

I didn't require much in the way of clothing for the trip, but decided to take my five-string banjo. Grandmother and I had never spent two days together, just the two of us, and I had reason to suppose that I might need to entertain myself at least part of the time. Actually, I didn't know what to expect. I was twenty-two and she was seventy-eight, and it occurred to me that Mable Curry and I were separated by an enormous gulf of time and experience. As a girl in the little Quaker community of Estacado, Texas, she had watched freight wagons pulled by spans of oxen arriving from Colorado City, loaded with lumber, cloth, flour, and sugar that had come by rail from Fort Worth. She had spent her entire childhood without ever seeing an automobile, airplane, electric light, indoor toilet, or telephone. What would we talk about? What did we have in common, really, other than pleasant memories and the tug of genetics? Two days in that big echoing house in Seminole might turn into an eternity of minutes and hours, and I might spend a lot of time on the front porch, playing my banjo for the mesquite trees in the vacant lot across the street.

Leaving Austin in the cool of morning, I drove west on Highway 290, winding my way through the Hill Country and pausing to absorb the charm of Blanco, Dripping Springs, Stonewall, Johnson City, and Fredericksburg. A citizen of West Texas could hardly make this drive without being seized by the feeling that this is what all of Texas should be: sleepy villages that had hardly changed since the 1920s, rivers that ran clear water, sturdy ranch houses made of native stone, and thrifty farmsteads surrounded by fruit trees, vineyards, beds of flowers, and bottomland fields bursting with green alfalfa. Nature had kissed this land and touched it with a gentle hand. If time had stopped here, it had stopped in a good place.

By the middle of the afternoon, I had left the land of bluebonnets and was driving down a highway of melting asphalt near Iraan. A blazing sun scowled upon gasping mesquites and rock-littered pastures, where fourteen-foot Aermotor windmills groaned in the breeze and pulled their precious load of water from aquifers deep in the ground. The highway stretched out in front of me until it vanished in a mirage dancing on the western horizon. Around six o'clock, I coasted into Seminole, with its wide streets laid out in straight lines on the points of the compass, its courthouse ensconced like a big box at the center of town, its churches of yellow brick, and its Piggly Wiggly supermarket, where Mrs. Tinnell bought groceries for Mrs. Curry's meals.

That is the way most people referred to her, as "Mrs. Curry." Very few people dared to suppose that they knew her well enough to slip into chummy first-name conversations. She wasn't chummy and strangers could sense it right away. My cousins and I often joked that when she entered heaven for the first time, God would address her as "Mrs. Curry," and she would call him "Young Man." She was "Grandmother" to her grandchildren, "Mother" to her daughters, and "Mrs. Curry" to

The Curry home in Seminole. 1973. Photo courtesy of Martha Marmaduke and Barbara Whitton.

the people of Seminole. Only her brothers and sister had license to use her first name.

North of the town square, I spotted a little Mexican restaurant on the east side of Main Street, turned right on Avenue E, and drove several blocks past drab houses and vacant lots grown up in weeds and beargrass. Then . . . there it was, just as I had remembered it, just as I had known it all my life: Grandmother Curry's house. My parents were married in the back yard. Joe Sherman's funeral was held inside the house in 1917. It stood out like an oasis amid a landscape of red sand and panting mesquite, an immaculate rambling white clapboard house with a broad porch on the south front, surrounded by a green lawn shaded by tall pines and Chinese elms.

The Chinese elm was one of several varieties of tree that had been popular with pioneering folk in West Texas, along with the tamarack and juniper, because of its ability to survive in a harsh climate. Without pruning and care, the Chinese elm tended to form an unruly scatter of limbs, permanently slouched away from the prevailing southwest wind, but Grandmother's elms had been pruned every spring and had achieved a height and graceful profile uncommon in West Texas. Flowers bloomed in beds below the porch and the whole compound, which took up half a city block, was enclosed inside a cinderblock fence that had recently been repainted a sparkling white. White and green were not natural colors in Gaines County, but they dominated here.

I parked in the driveway on the west side of the house, beneath a huge juniper tree that I had climbed as a boy, and rang the doorbell. Moments later, Grandmother appeared, showing a radiant smile of pearly white teeth, all her own, and a pair of light blue eyes behind austere rimless glasses. Depending on the circumstance, those eyes could sparkle with mirth and intelligence, or scorch the paint off a wall ten feet away. In our youth, my cousins and I had seen both sides and lived in fear of the latter. She wore a dress that reached to mid-calf and a pair of black shoes with a raised heel, and as always, she was perfectly groomed. If she had ever worn a pair of pants or casual shoes in her whole life, nobody in my family had a record of it, and I couldn't recall ever seeing her hair in disarray. The skin on her face was not the skin of an old woman, but had the translucent sheen of alabaster. At the age of seventy-eight, she had no wrinkles, sags, bags, or lines. She was still a beautiful woman. She was smaller than I remembered, maybe only five-feet four, but when we embraced I recognized her scent, a pleasant blend of soap, perfume, coffee, and bacon.

She moved into this house as a bride in 1911 and had never left it, a remarkable achievement in a society as restless and mobile as ours. The original house sat on several acres of land where a windmill provided water for the house as well as for chickens and several milk cows, a big garden, and an orchard of fruit trees. It had been a smaller house back then, with rooms added when children came and when the cattle market allowed the purchase of lumber and hardware.

I had arrived just in time for supper and Mrs. Tennill had already set two places at Grandmother's big rectangular dining table, which looked out on the green expanse of the back yard. We bowed our heads and

Grandmother said the blessing, then Mrs. Tennill brought out the feast she had spent all afternoon preparing: fried steak, mashed potatoes and gravy, fried okra, boiled squash, and her homemade chow-chow relish. Both ladies watched with pleasure as I devoured my food. Smiling, Grandmother said, "It's always good to see a man eat." Mrs. Tennill nodded her agreement.

After supper, Mrs. Tennill cleaned up the kitchen and went home, leaving me and Grandmother alone in the big house. We moved into more comfortable chairs in the living room and Grandmother saw my banjo case beside the door. She asked if I would play something, so I pulled it out and played several folksongs I had learned from records by Pete Seeger and the Weavers. When I sang "Irene, Good Night," I was surprised to hear Grandmother singing along in a creaky alto voice. She asked me to do some old cowboy songs and she sang along on those too.

We sang and talked until nine-thirty, then she said good night and went into her room. I drifted into the library on the west side of the house. Buck Curry died reading a book in this room in 1947 and Grandmother had kept it just as he'd left it, with his handmade spurs sitting on one of the shelves. My cousins and I had played in Buck Curry's library many times but I had never given much thought to the three walls that were filled, floor to ceiling, with books. Now, as a university student, I took a closer look.

I went to a shelf that held a number of old leather-bound volumes, pulled one out, and saw that it was part of a twelve-volume set of the complete writings of George Washington, edited by Jarred Sparks. I knew enough about old books to recognize it as a valuable collector's piece, a set you would expect to find in a first-rate university library but not in a private collection in Gaines County, Texas. This volume, and many others in the collection, carried a sticker in the front that said, "Claitor's Book Store, Baton Rouge, La." Grampy Buck's part of Texas had produced very few bookstores, so he had done most of his book-buying by mail.

As I browsed through the books, it began to dawn on me that my Grandfather Curry had assembled a very impressive library that revealed an astounding range of interests. There were books on geology, meteorology, banking, agriculture, range management, ethnology, and archeology. He had put together a good collection on New Mexico history, another on Indians of the Southwest, and another on exploration of the American West: Fremont, Long, De Soto, Zebulon Pike, Josiah Gregg, and others. Another section contained books on American presidents and statesmen, and still another covered the American Civil War. There were books on the history of Greece, Rome, Egypt, the Jews, and several American states. He had compiled an excellent Texana collection, covering early exploration, the war of Texas Independence, and the frontier period; Indians, cowboys, trail drivers, buffalo hunters, ranchers, generals, and statesmen; texts by Yoakum, Brown, Duval, Wilbarger, Dobie, Webb, Perry, Holden, Billy Dixon, and J. Evetts Haley.

I plucked J. Evetts Haley's biography of Charles Goodnight off the shelf and thumbed through it. I had heard about this book, a classic of Texas literature, but had never read it. On the first page, I saw a note Buck Curry had written in black ink: "B. B. Curry's book. Bought from

Grandmother Curry in the library, with picture of Buck behind her. 1970. Photo courtesy of Martha Marmaduke and Barbara Whitton.

J. Evetts Haley 1937." I turned to the title page and saw that it was a first edition, published in 1936. Fascinated, I settled into the chair and began reading. On page forty-nine I found a checkmark in the right margin, beside a paragraph that began, "On their way out to the open country they came to where a man named Sherman had settled on Stagg Prairie, in the western edge of Parker County." My eyes rose from the page and I stared in wonder. This was the story about the death of my great-great grandmother, Martha Sherman. As a child, I had heard it from my mother, but I had never known when or where it occurred, or if it was more than a family folktale. Now here it was in Buck Curry's book, and if he hadn't made that checkmark in the margin, I might never have found it.

That discovery in Grampy Buck's library was the starting point of a research project that has covered almost four decades and has taken final form in this book. It has been my effort to reconstruct the story of my mother's family in West Texas and to restore faded portraits of family members I never knew, and who seemed to have some desire not to be known.

Chapter Three: The Quakers

John Graves has observed that "most of West Texas accords ill with the Saxon nostalgia for cool, green, dew-wet landscapes" (John Graves 1960: 5), and any journey that begins in Austin and ends in Seminole or Lubbock provokes the question, "Why did people ever come here?" Why did they pass through the softer, greener counties in central Texas and keep following the sun until, two hundred miles west of Fort Worth, they climbed the caprock escarpment and looked out on that vast expanse of featureless prairie known as the Llano Estacado, or Staked Plains?

Even the Comanches didn't spend much time on the Llano, but used it as a temporary refuge from the U.S. military. When the soldiers followed them out into the dry wastes of the Llano, it usually turned out badly for the boys in blue. The Comanches survived because they knew the location of every spring and hole of water. In dry years, they cut small slits into the jugular veins of their horses and drank the blood. The soldiers—those who didn't perish from thirst—wandered their way back to civilization, having gained a hard education about the Llano Estacado.

Today, the Llano is home to more than a million people, most of them residing in Amarillo, Lubbock, Midland, and Odessa. Irrigation water from the Ogallala Aquifer has transformed the Llano into a very productive breadbasket region, yielding enormous quantities of cotton, corn silage, feed grains, wheat, wine grapes, and sunflowers. The discovery of oil and natural gas has broadened the economic base and provided employment for thousands. If you happen to be driving between Amarillo and Lubbock in August of a good crop year, you might mistake this fertile tabletop for the countryside around Modesto, California. Technology and settlement have gone a long distance toward defanging the Llano, muting the qualities that caused members of Coronado's 1540 expedition to exclaim that they were passing through a land "as bare of landmarks as if we were surrounded by the sea." (Jenkins 1986: xi)

But make that same drive in a drought year and you might see snowplows pushing dunes of red sand off the highways and tumbleweed cannonballs snapping power lines and laying barbed wire fences flat on the ground—things my mother remembered during the drought of the 1930s. In February, you might step outside and feel the slash of Arctic winds that can freeze water in minutes, winds that penetrate human flesh like a razor and evoke thoughts of a frozen hell on Mars.

In 1849 Captain Randolph Marcy saw the face of nature's wrath on the Llano. After his expedition along the Canadian River had endured broiling heat, bad water, a pestilence of biting insects, and a barrage of hailstones that had dented their steel helmets, he wrote this bitter assessment of the place: "The great Zahara of North America . . . a timeless, desolate waste of uninhabitable solitude, which always has been, and must continue uninhabited forever." (Jenkins 1986: 2)

So why, I wondered, did the Underhills, Grandmother Curry's grandparents, leave Huron County, Ohio, in 1881 and move to Estacado, Texas, a tiny settlement huddled upon the eastern fringe of the Llano? The audacity of the move takes the breath away. It suggests either courage or ignorance on a grand scale, and maybe both. These Quakers were the very antithesis of our notions of frontiersmen. John W. Murry, the editor of Estacado's newspaper, described them this way:

> "The Quakers were a peculiar people. The women wore full skirts and bonnets. The men wore wide-brimmed hats and tight fitting trousers, and rolled their long hair at the ends in William

Penn style. These people, not used to the ways of the Gentiles, were sorely tried by their cursing, drinking, and gambling, and were irritated by the cowboys, who constantly courted and often won the hearts and hands of their lovely daughters. The Quakers could hardly endure this." (Jenkins 1986: 150)

Here is another description of them:

"Their peculiarities of speech in the use of thee and thou, instead of you, marked them from other religious groups. [In West Texas] they hoped to establish this religion in its purer form, isolated from other religious sects, so that their children, being associated with none other than [members of the Society of] Friends, would naturally marry those of like belief, thereby keeping their religion as the original founders hoped that it would remain." (Spikes and Ellis 1952: 259)

The Quakers were usually described as quiet, gentle, self-effacing folk who read their books, said their prayers, and tended their fields. Yet the history of the American frontier contains several examples of Quakers who popped up in odd places, doing things that hardly seemed to fit the stereotype. During the administration of President U. S. Grant, the Society of Friends lobbied hard for more humane treatment of the Plains Indians and played an active role in Grant's Peace Policy. In 1869, Lawrie Tatum, "an unimaginative but courageous and sensible Quaker," left the comforts of home and took up his duties at Fort Sill as the agent of the Comanches, Kiowas, and Kiowa-Apaches—the most violent and troublesome of all the plains tribes. (Wallace and Hoebel 1952: 314)

"Tatum felt that God had called him to this new work, about which he knew nothing. . . . The Friends believed that kindness and honesty would solve the Indian problem." But the Plains tribes made a shambles of Tatum's efforts and "he soon came to the conclusion that force was the only kind of treatment that some Indians understood and respected." (Wallace and Hoebel 1952: 314)

This drew harsh criticism from Tatum's fellow Quakers, and in 1873 he was removed from his post, replaced by J. M. Haworth, "a thoroughgoing Quaker and a firm believer in the Peace Policy." (Wallace and Hoebel 1952: 318) Under Haworth's leadership, the Peace Policy careened into the failure it was destined to be from the start, a collision between the idealism of gentle people and the cold fact that his wards just enjoyed being pirates.

I don't recall my mother or grandmother ever venturing an opinion on why the Underhills went west, so I made my own speculations. As members of the Society of Friends, they were pacifists and refused service in the Civil War. Perhaps by 1881 their refusal to serve had begun to sour their relations with their neighbors. The novelist in me concocted scenes on the streets of Greenwich, Ohio: frigid stares from the "Gentiles," as the Quakers referred to those not of their faith; snarls and whispers of "coward, traitor!"; Quaker children threatened by young bullies who, at the age of thirteen or fourteen, had reached that point in human development where cruelty and ignorance overlap. It made a plausible script that would explain why farmers would uproot their families and walk away from one of the most fertile farming regions in the entire world.

On the other hand, the Underhills might have had more mundane reasons for leaving the Midwest. Bennett Kerr, my mother's sister, said that the Underhills had prospered as farmers in Ohio, but a doctor had told them that their daughter Emma couldn't survive another winter in the Midwest, so they went west for a healthier climate. (Mike Harter letter, 1998)

The man behind this migration of Quakers was Paris Cox, a native of North Carolina. "As a young man he was conscripted by the Confederate States of America to serve in the Civil War. Having been taught Quaker principles concerning peace and not bearing arms, he bought his exemption, which was legal at that time, and migrated north and west." (Jenkins 1986: 173)

15

In the late 1870s he joined a group of buffalo hunters in Texas—a peculiar occupation for a pacifist Quaker—and explored the unsettled frontier from the Pecos River up into Kansas. He was particularly charmed by the prairie landscape in Crosby County, on the Llano Estacado, where no one had ever attempted to build a permanent settlement, not even the leathery Comanches who knew its moods better than anyone. Cox declared, "Here by the will of God will be my home." (Jenkins 1986: 173)

A decade later, it became painfully clear that Paris Cox was more of a poet than an engineer, and that he had seen West Texas in what must have been one of the most bountiful years it had known since the days of Noah. He acquired eighty square miles of land in Crosby and Lubbock Counties, then traveled through the Midwest, selling his Texas land to adventurous Quakers at fifty cents per acre. In the spring of 1879 he and three families left Indianapolis and established their colony in Crosby County: Estacado, Texas.

We have the recollections of one of the early settlers, J. W. Hunt, who saw the High Plains as a child and later became the founding president of McMurry College in Abilene:

> "With vast wonder, [we] beheld the virgin land. No plow had ever depraved its sod. No fences marked boundaries cut from its majestic sweep of rolling terrain. Copious rains had fallen. The prairie grass, lush and green, covered the land. The yucca stalk, crowned with festoons of white blossoms, grew in picturesque profusion, like a budding Aaron's rod a million times multiplied. . . . The landscape, dotted with little lakes gleaming in the morning sun, seemed a vast emerald shield embossed with gems and silver. 'Well,' said father at last in his deep voice, 'we are on the Plains.' My mother sat on the wagon seat with steady, unfathomable eyes of the frontier woman, gazing into infinity; and said nothing." (Jenkins 1986: v)

We will never know what Mr. Hunt's mother was thinking, but one suspects she might have been wondering, "What are we doing here?" To a farming man, that "infinity" she saw spread out in all directions meant an abundance of cheap land—land whose fertility had been tested and confirmed, land that wasn't choked with trees and brush that had to be cleared and burned, land that could bring pride and respectability. But Mrs. Hunt must have sensed the terrible loneliness of a place where the only sound was the ceaseless moan of the wind.

Paris Cox and his group lived in tents through the first winter. Their nearest source of supply lay in Fort Griffin, 170 miles to the southeast. They dug a well and plowed some ground for crops, but by that time:

> "…three of the families could stand the solitude no longer and gathered their belongings into their wagons and drove away, leaving one lone family—that of Paris Cox, his wife, and two little boys to continue the battle. Who can tell what that wife and mother felt as she saw the wagons fade into the distance and turned back into the tent with her two little boys?

> "In the following April [1880] came the hard spring winds and one day while the hired hand was gone for supplies and the husband for wood, a western gale grew in fury until the tent began to give way. In terror the mother seized upon the lower edge and strove to hold it down. She was lifted from her feet, but she struggled until, with a loud report, the tent burst asunder and was torn from its fastening and blown across the prairie. That night she and the little ones had no canopy but the starry sky and the gale howled while the wild animal life barked and screamed through the hideous night. They were learning what frontier life was." (Quillen manuscript, nd: 3–4)

My relatives, the Harvey Underhill and George Singer families, came the following year, in 1881. They joined a group of Quakers in Iowa, boarded a train in Kansas City, and with each family member allowed two hundred pounds of baggage, rode to Fort Worth, where they saw piles of buffalo bones beside the railroad tracks. They transferred to wagons that took them to the last outpost of civilization at Fort Griffin, near present-day Albany, where they bought provisions for the final leg of their journey. There, Perlina Underhill, my great-grandmother, saw Indians for the first time, probably Tonkawa scouts attached to the military. She wore a red hat that her mother had knitted and was alarmed at the way the Indians stared it. She would have been thirteen at the time. (Mike Harter letter, 1998; Bennett Kerr interview, 2004)

John Alley gives us a description of the fort as the Underhills might have seen it:

"Fort Griffin was at this time the furtherest western outpost. A small company of soldiers had been sent there to guard Texas against depredations of the Indians and to otherwise preserve peace. A few ranchmen and honorable buffalo hunters made this headquarters. But for the most part, Fort Griffin's citizenship was made up of the scum of the earth—desperadoes, fugitives from justice—who plied many trades, honorable and dishonorable. There were saloons and dance halls, gambling and drinking, and all kinds of crime. Also, a small tribe of friendly Tonkawa Indians camped near the town." (John Alley article, 1932: part 7)

By the time the Underhill wagon reached the Llano Estacado, Harvey was having second thoughts and wondered if they should turn around and go back. Anna, his wife, a round, jolly woman who always seemed able to produce cookies from the pockets of her apron, quoted a passage from the Bible, saying, "Unless a man put his hand to the plow and looketh not back, he shall not enter the kingdom." (Mike Harter letter, 1998)

That settled the matter and they drove on to Estacado, where the family lived in a tent until they could build a house. Great-Grandmother

Sherman hated living in a tent, as no one had any privacy. (Bennett Kerr interview, 2004) Once they became established, Harvey farmed and operated a hotel. By at least one account, Harvey was Estacado's first hotelkeeper. (Spikes and Ellis 1952: 34)

In 1998 my cousin Martha Marmaduke located a photograph of Harvey Underhill in a pictorial history of Lubbock, Texas, and to my knowledge, it is the only one in existence. It shows a man with longish hair and strong features, pale blue or green eyes, and a "Menonite" beard with no mustache. In those days, people didn't feel compelled to smile for the camera and as a result, the photographic record of our forebears often portrays them as a scowling, unhappy lot. Harvey Underhill wasn't mugging for the camera, but his mouth holds the hint of a smile, suggesting the he might have been a pleasant fellow with a

Harvey Underhill,
date unknown.
Photo courtesy of the
Southwest Collection,
Texas Tech University.

sense of humor. It is noteworthy that this photograph showed neither the "William Penn" style of hair nor a wide-brimmed black hat which Editor Murray included in his description of the Quakers. Maybe Harvey Underhill wasn't as strict as some of his neighbors. As we will see, two of his daughters married outside the faith.

The town of Estacado grew and prospered. The original tents and dugout houses were replaced by wooden structures made of lumber freighted by ox teams from the railhead at Colorado City, 120 miles to the south. In an 1887 issue of the *Crosby County News*, the editor gave this assessment of his neighbors:

> "These [Quaker] people are temperate, industrious, law abiding, kind hearted and honest in their deportment and dealings, and being long in the majority, have impressed their excellent principles upon the community. They believe in education, and the fine school, now the pride of our colony in Estacado,

Quaker schoolgirls in Estacado, 1886. Top, left to right: Laura Lewis, Emma Hunt, Lina Underhill, Lydia Cox, Lillie Cox. Bottom Row, left to right: Allie Paxon, Katie Conroe, Hulda Cox, Elva Lewis. Photo courtesy of Panhandle-Plains Historical Museum.

is the result of their enlightened enterprise. They came here first and subdued the wilderness, exposing the fallacy of the unproductiveness of the plains." (Jenkins 1986: 141)

By that time, though, the Quakers had some "Gentile" neighbors, mostly ranchers and cowboys who had come west to graze herds of cattle on the strong grasses that grew on the tableland above the caprock. In that same issue of the *Crosby County News*, immediately beneath the passage quoted above, there is a listing of county officials. The County Commissioner for the Third Precinct is listed as Joe Sherman.

Joe Sherman was Grandmother Curry's father, and if there was ever a man who fit the Quaker definition of a Gentile, it was Joe Sherman.

Chapter Four: Martha Sherman

Mother told me stories about Joe Sherman, but he always seemed a man who occupied the shadows. He died when Mother was a small child and, for reasons that remained obscure to me until many years later, his death was shrouded in mystery. When Mother spoke of that event, her voice dropped into a hushed tone that caused me to lean forward and listen to every word. She was four years old at the time, which would have placed the event in 1916 or 1917. She heard an odd sound coming from her mother's bedroom. Alarmed, Anna Beth broke one of Mrs. Curry's iron rules and entered the room without knocking. Inside, she saw her mother sitting in front of her dressing table, her face buried in her hands. She was crying.

Anna Beth went to her and said, "Mother, what's wrong?" Startled, Mable turned on the child and screamed, "Get out! Get out!"

Mother ran out of the room, terrified and certain that something dreadful had come over the house. Later, she learned that her grandfather, Joe Sherman, had died from a gunshot wound. It was an event that brought such disgrace to the Shermans and Currys that no one in my family ever discussed it. Fifty years after it happened, Grandmother Curry still wouldn't talk about it with her own daughters. I would eventually piece the story back together, but without any help from my Sherman kin. Grandmother Curry and her brothers received my questions with a stiff silence, a quality my mother often referred to as "the Sherman Chill." No one had ever accused the Shermans of having loose tongues.

And then there was the story about Joe Sherman's mother. Anna Beth told me that when Joe Sherman was a boy, his mother was killed by Indians. Typically, Mother omitted certain details, such as when, where, why, and what kind of Indians, making it the kind of story a boy might relate to his friends at school, who would dismiss as fiction. I was never sure of that myself until that evening in the summer of 1966, when I found the check-marked passage in J. Evetts Haley's biography of Charles Goodnight:

> "On their way out to the open country [the Comanches] came to where a man by the name of Sherman had settled on Stagg Prairie, in the western edge of Parker County. . . . It was raining heavily as five warriors dismounted, drove the family out, seized Mrs. Sherman, tied her to the ground, violated her, and shot two or three arrows into her body. She lived until the next day, giving birth to a dead child." (Haley 1936: 49-50)

This was the story Mother had told me years before, only now I had a place and time: Parker or Palo Pinto County, Texas, in November of 1860. Later, armed with that information, I went to the Texas Archives in downtown Austin and began poring over crumbling newspapers, files of letters, books on frontier history, and microfilm records. I soon realized that the death of Martha Sherman, a story that had lain half-forgotten in the memory of my family, was a major news event on the Texas frontier in the winter of 1860-61. It was widely reported at the time and has been mentioned in a number of books since then. And it eventually included some important figures in Texas history: Charles Goodnight, Sam Houston, Sul Ross, Quanah Parker, and Cynthia Ann Parker. It also had a powerful effect on a two-year old boy who saw it happen, Joe Sherman.

By the fall of 1860, the line of Anglo-American settlement in Texas had pushed west of Fort Worth, and Parker, Young, Jack, and

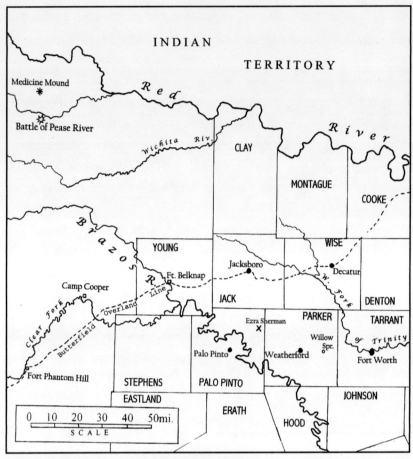

North Central Texas, 1860. Map by Mike Harter

Palo Pinto Counties had become the cutting edge of the frontier. Ezra Sherman and his wife Martha had settled on land west of Weatherford, on the Parker-Palo Pinto county line, a very dangerous place to be, as it turned out.

The hostile Indians, including several bands of the notorious Comanche tribe, had been resettled on reservations north of the Red River in Indian Territory (later Oklahoma), but some of them grew restless for the old ways of raiding and plundering. In November, Chief Peta Nocona led a band of Comanches and Kiowas on a rampage that took them down to the settlements west of Weatherford.

Sam Houston had come out of retirement to serve as governor. Raised in Tennessee, Houston had enjoyed pleasant relations with the mild mannered Cherokees and did not share the vehement anti-Indian sentiment of many Texans. But as reports of Comanche depredations continued to pour in from the frontier, he called for federal troops and sent Texas Rangers to the frontier, under the command of Captain Sul Ross, who later served as governor of Texas. (Haley 1936: 48-9)

In late November, the Comanches killed several people near Jacksboro, then moved on to Lost Valley, the home ground of Charles Goodnight and Oliver Loving. Loving later achieved fame as a trail driver, and served as the model for Augustus McCray in Larry McMurtry's novel *Lonesome Dove*. The Comanches killed a man named Brown, cut off his nose, and "lanced him in every part of the body, and moved on to Stagg Prairie, where they found Martha Sherman in her house with three children." (Haley 1936: 49)

The dozens of accounts of the incident differ in some of the details; Haley says Ezra Sherman was gone when the Comanches arrived, others say he was there. I am inclined to trust the accounts given by Mrs. Charles Haydon of Plainview, Texas, who heard it from her father, William Henry Cheairs. William Cheairs was Joe Sherman's half-brother, eight years old at the time of the murder and an eyewitness.

> "At noon, Grandmother Sherman was fixing dinner when she noticed a bunch of men on horseback, whom she took to be Indians, a bunch of about twenty-five or thirty. She told Mr. Sherman, her husband, that they were Indians but he told her not to be frightened, as they were only cowboys. So they forgot all about it, thinking they were cowboys, when all at once a chief rode up with five others and faced the house.

> "Mr. Sherman had no gun, having traded it recently for an ox yoke, and he went out to treat them kindly, as he thought they would not harm the family, but the chief raised in his stirrups

and whistled aloud. The rest of the Indians, who were hidden, surrounded the house. They all dismounted from their horses and went into the house, slapped Grandma several times and told Mr. Sherman to take her and the papoose [Joe Sherman] and leave. [The Indians] then turned the table over, which had dinner on it.

"Mr. Sherman took Grandma and the three children [Henry, Mary, and Joe] and started to a neighbor's house, a distance of about two miles. When about halfway, the chief overtook them and took Grandma away from Mr. Sherman. [The chief] took her by the hair of the head and dragged her a quarter mile, beat her, violated her, took the pins from her clothes and stuck them in her flesh. Then he scalped her and left her to die, taking the scalp, the family Bible, and a man's coat with him.

"When Mr. Sherman reached the neighbor's house, he got a gun and went back, but the Indians were gone. He found Grandma a little ways from the house. He pulled the pins from her flesh and tied a red bandana around her head. She called for water and Mr. Sherman carried it to her in his hat. Then, picking her up, he carried her to the house. Her baby was born prematurely that night, dead. She stayed in the house until her death three days later. (Haydon 1925: 1-2; Haydon 1965: 1)

The incident made news all over the frontier, even in Clarksville, in northeast Texas, where *The Clarksville Standard* added a few grisly details:

"On Mr. Sherman returning to the house, he found his wife gone but was attracted by her groans. He found her crawling toward the creek in search of water, and horrible to relate, her

entire scalp was taken off and an arrow sticking in her side. . . .
The horrible manner in which Mrs. Sherman was murdered is
appalling to the stoutest heart."

This account in the Clarksville paper also added an interesting detail.
One of the members of the raiding party wore "a red flannel shirt, which
dress is wholly unusual for Comanches" and "spoke in plain English."
Before she died, the report continues, Mrs. Sherman told friends and
family that Red Shirt "declared his determination to take a spree into
Weatherford on Christmas day." (*Clarksville Standard,* December 1860)

Other versions of the story say nothing about a red flannel shirt, but
have one of the raiders being a man with green eyes and red hair. More
on that later.

In her book on the family of Quanah and Cynthia Ann Parker, Jo
Ella Powell Exley writes:

"The Sherman murder, the latest in a series of atrocities, was
the last straw for the settlers in the [Fort] Belknap, Palo Pinto,
and Jacksboro area. Some forted up by joining together in the
strongest and best protected log cabins. Others left the country
in droves. . . . At the same time, the men of the community,
outraged by twenty-three murders in the past few months,
decided to rid the country of the Comanches forever. A major
expedition was planned." (Exley 2001: 145)

Charles Goodnight, a young man living not far from the Sherman
place, got news of the raid around dark. "I started immediately to
warn the neighborhood and get together enough men to follow them
and make a fight. The rain was falling in torrents and continued
to do so all night. I believe it was one of the darkest nights I ever
experienced." He rode all night, alerting the neighbors, including a
man named Lynn, whom he found sitting in front of an open fire,
curing a fresh Indian scalp on a stick. At daylight, Goodnight and a

Charles Goodnight as young man, near the age when he found Mrs. Sherman's Bible. Photo courtesy of Panhandle-Plains Historical Museum.

group of men followed the trail of the Indians out of Loving's Valley, and for several days trailed them northward to the Pease River, near present-day Crowell. There, they gave up the chase and returned to Palo Pinto County for supplies and reinforcements. "A total of twenty-three persons had been reported killed in the raids, and the atrocious nature of the killings struck terror into everyone not inured to border life." Residents of the frontier fled their homes and took refuge in Weatherford and Camp Cooper. On December 13, 1860, a contingent of Texas Rangers under the command of Captain Sul Ross joined dragoons from Camp Cooper and a group of local volunteers under the command of Jack Cureton. The small army rode north toward the Pease River with Goodnight acting as scout. Along the way, "Goodnight picked up Mrs. Sherman's Bible, where it had been dropped by the Indians. It had fallen with the lids closed and was undamaged by the rain." (Haley 1936: 49-53)

Why had the Comanches bothered to steal the family Bible? Goodnight explained, "The Indians knew as well as we did the resistance paper had against bullets. . . . When they robbed houses they invariably took all the books they could find, using the paper to pack their shields." (Haley 1936:53)

Only minutes after picking up Mrs. Sherman's Bible, Goodnight found fresh sign that the Comanches were close by. Ross's Rangers went thundering into the camp, catching the enemy completely by surprise. Goodnight continues the story:

> "The fight, which lasted only a few minutes, continued on the plain until all the Indians were killed. Ross had a hand-to-hand fight with the chief and killed him. [Not Peta Nocona, as Goodnight and others thought at the time]. One of the squaws was riding a good iron-gray horse, and in spite of the fact that she had an infant in her arms, kept up with the six or eight bucks. I understand that Ross ordered one of his Rangers, Tom Kelliher, to take charge of her, fearing, I suppose, that the regulars [soldiers] would come upon her, as they had the others, and kill her. To the credit of the old Texas Rangers, not one of them shot a squaw that day." (Haley 1936: 56)

Even by frontier standards, November and December of 1860 had been one of the most gruesome thirty-day periods on record, with quantities of blood spilled on both sides. The Comanches had had their sport, and now the Texans had evened the score, "smiting them hip and thigh," as Texas author John Graves expressed it in his account of Mrs. Sherman's murder. (John Graves 1960: 139)

Mr. Graves, whom I met in 1973 and with whom I still exchange occasional letters, passed harsh judgment on Ezra Sherman, saying that he was naive and ignorant of the cold realities of frontier life. Sherman didn't understand that Comanches on the war trail "lacked the aspect that a man would want to see in his luncheon guests," and had no business bringing a wife and three children out to the edge of the frontier when he "had failed to furnish himself with firearms." (John Graves 1960: 133).

With news of Comanche depredations on the minds and lips of every pale-skinned resident of Parker and Palo Pinto counties, how could Ezra Sherman have *traded his rifle for an ox yoke*? What kind of world did he think he was occupying? Justice would have been served if Ezra had paid with his own life, but fate denied him that option, forcing him instead to see in horrible vivid detail the consequences of his careless decision. We can only imagine the thoughts that burned through his mind as he covered Martha's bald bleeding head with his bandana and offered her a drink of water from his hat. What could he say? "I'm sorry. I just didn't realize . . . I should have known . . ." It was too late for words, and after burying his wife, Ezra became a man haunted by memories that wouldn't go away.

In a 1963 interview with Edith Standhardt, my great-uncle, Roy Sherman, said:

> "Ezra, filled with remorse because he had not protected his family, volunteered for the Confederate Army, although he was over the age to be called up. He fought at the Battle of Gettysburg and was severely wounded. Later, he was discharged as unfit for further service, and returned home. The wounds broke loose and he lived only four days after reaching home." (Roy Sherman interview, 1963)

Uncle Roy had a steel-trap memory for details, even in his old age. I checked his recollections of other incidents against newspaper stories and historical records, and he was seldom wrong. But on this occasion, either his memory had lapsed or else he was repeating a family story that had given a shred of dignity to Ezra's last days on earth, probably the latter.

The yellowed records of the Confederate Army in Texas tell a different story. Ezra enlisted in "Company A, 21 Reg't Texas Infantry" on March

3, 1862. In June of 1863, one month before the Battle of Gettysburg, he was reported "present sick" somewhere near Houston; then in October, "absent sick, furlough Parker Co. since Aug. 25, '63." The regimental return dated January 2, 1864 states, "Died of disease, Parker Co." (Texas State Archives, Austin)

The fact is, Ezra didn't fight at Gettysburg and never even left Texas. Though he probably hoped to redeem himself on the battlefield, that was denied him. Ezra Sherman wasn't a man who had much good luck. A photograph of him in the Palo Pinto County history book shows a rather handsome young man wearing a military jacket with the collar turned up around the line of his jaw. His pale blue eyes, deeply set into their sockets, stare straight into the camera and suggest bewilderment and an emptiness of spirit. (Palo Pinto Historical Commission 1986: 474)

Ezra Sherman carried his disgrace and shame to the grave, but as Mike Harter has observed, even if Ezra had possessed a gun on that

Ezra Sherman in Confederate uniform, 1863. Photo courtesy of Martha Marmaduke and Barbara Whitton.

fateful day, it probably would have only deepened the tragedy. "Had he used it, Peta Nocona likely would have massacred the whole family. The Comanches apparently wanted to humiliate him. They succeeded tenfold. Poor Ezra was shamed forever." (Mike Harter letter, 2004)

But there was more to the Battle of Pease River. After the Texans had won the field and dispatched the warriors who had murdered Martha Sherman, a surprise awaited them when they took a closer look at that Comanche woman they had captured.

Chapter Five: Cynthia Ann

"The squaw was in terrible grief," Goodnight told his biographer, the young J. Evetts Haley:

> "I thought I would try to console her and make her understand that she would not be hurt. When I got near her I noticed that she had blue eyes and light hair, which had been cut short. It was a little difficult to distinguish her blond features, as her face and hands were extremely dirty. . . " (Haley 1936: 57)

Astonished, Goodnight realized that he was looking into the eyes of an Anglo woman who had been kidnapped by the Comanches and had adopted their ways; and she was holding a bronze-faced baby that had been sired by Chief Peta Nocona himself. She was, of course, Cynthia Ann Parker, and her story is one of the best known in all of Texas history.

Cynthia Ann had lived with her family at Fort Parker, on the headwaters of the Navasota River near present-day Groesbeck, and in May of 1836 tensions ran high between the settlers and the Indians, a mixture of northern Comanches and their Kiowa allies. Agents of the Mexican government had been stirring the pot in hopes of gaining advantage over the Texans and Americans. Around nine o'clock on the morning of May 19, two hundred Indians appeared in front of the fort.

"The fort was at that time occupied by six men and several women and children. Four other men, belonging to the fort, had gone out to do field work. The Indians presented a white flag, and sent two of their number to the fort, to say that they were friendly, and desired to treat. One of the inmates, Benjamin Parker, went out to see the main body of the Indians, but soon returned and reported unfavorably. However, he went out a second time, hoping to make peace, but was surrounded and killed. Those in the fort attempted to fly, but the most of them were cruelly massacred, and their bodies mutilated. The fort was then plundered, and the savages retreated, with some of the women and children as prisoners." (Yoakum 1935: 170)

Among the captives were nine-year old Cynthia Ann and her brother. Her parents dead, the girl lived among the Comanches as a slave and chore girl. But she learned the Comanche language and adopted their ways and became the wife of an important man, Peta Nocona, with whom she had three children: two sons (Quanah and Pee-nah) and a daughter (Prairie Flower). By 1860, when she was recaptured by Ross's party, she had long ago been given up for dead. Yet the story of her kidnapping had been part of the folklore on the frontier and Ross was convinced that the captive and Cynthia Ann Parker, now a woman of thirty-four, were one and the same.

At Camp Cooper, Ross sent word to her uncle, Isaac Parker, and asked him to come and speak with the woman.

"Upon the arrival of Colonel Parker at Fort Cooper interrogations were made her through the Mexican interpreter, for she remembered not one word of English, respecting her identity; but she had forgotten absolutely everything, apparently, at all connected with her family or past history. In despair of being unable to reach a conclusion Colonel Parker was about to leave when he said: 'The name of my niece was Cynthia

Ann.' The sound of the once familiar name, doubtless the last lingering memento of the old home at the fort, seemed to touch a responsive chord in her nature, when a sign of intelligence lighted up her countenance, as memory by some mystic inspiration resumed its cunning as she looked up, and patting her breast, said: 'Cynthia Ann! Cynthia Ann!' There was now no longer any doubt as to her identity with the little girl lost and mourned so long. It was in reality Cynthia Ann Parker—but, oh, so changed!" (Wilbarger 1889: 340)

The Parkers were overjoyed at this return of the prodigal child. Cynthia Ann and her baby, Prairie Flower, were taken to Isaac's home, where she "sought every opportunity to escape and had to be closely watched for some time." On their way to the Parker home in Birdville, they stopped in Fort Worth.

Cynthia Ann Parker and Prairie Flower. Photo courtesy Panhandle-Plains Historical Museum.

"There, after much difficulty, Cynthia Ann was persuaded to have her picture taken with Prairie Flower. Word spread about the recapture of Cynthia Ann, and she and Prairie Flower had become celebrities. According to Medora Robinson Turner, who was a child at the time, all the students were let out of school so that they could see the captives, who had been taken to Turner and Daggett's general store. Medora describes Cynthia Ann and the scene that took place: 'She stood on a large wooden box, she was bound with rope, she was not dressed in Indian costume, but wore a torn calico dress. Her hair was bronzed by the sun. Her face was tanned, and she made a pathetic figure as she stood there, viewing the crowds that swarmed about her. The tears were streaming down her face, and she was muttering in the Indian language.' The children asked the principal what she was saying, and he told them that she was asking to be taken back to her people [the Comanches]." (Exley 2001: 170-1)

Gradually, she began speaking English again, and during the Civil War, she learned to spin, weave, and perform domestic chores. (Wilbarger 1889: 341) "Cynthia Ann still clung to her Indian customs. When a member of the family died, she would sing a plaintive mourning song and slash her body with a knife. The family would try to dissuade her from hurting herself but to no avail." (Exley 2001: 177)

Cynthia Ann also grieved for her two sons, fearing that they were being mistreated by the Comanches, who were never kind to orphans. She still had little Prairie Flower, who had learned English and had found playmates in the community, but in 1864 the little girl contracted pneumonia and died. Jo Ella Powell Exley states that Cynthia Ann lived another six years, dying in 1870. (Exley 2001: 179)

J. Evetts Haley placed her death shortly after the death of her baby, and gave the episode a poetic conclusion:

"Yearning for the treeless Plains where Nocona and her sons still hunted the buffalo, and sinking with grief and loneliness, she died, apparently of a broken heart, in 1864—an expatriate among people of her own blood. Her tragic story is a part of the Texas tradition." (Haley 1936: 59)

Cynthia Ann's story was actually a double tragedy, as she was twice captured and twice wrenched away from her loved ones. It has fascinated five generations of storytellers and poets, and has been beautifully rendered in a song, "White Women's Clothes," written by Lubbock poet Andy Wilkinson, a grand-nephew of Charles Goodnight. (*Charlie*

Quanah Parker, Comanche chief. Photo courtesy of Panhandle-Plains Historical Museum.

Goodnight: His Life in Poetry and Song, Grey Horse Press, 1994) In the song, Cynthia Ann's lines are belted out by a full-voiced teenage girl from Lubbock named Natalie Maines, who a few years later became the lead singer for The Dixie Chicks.

There is some dispute about whether or not Quanah was present at the Battle of Pease River, but there is no doubt that he survived and grew into manhood. This son of Cynthia Ann and Chief Peta Nocona became the last of the great Comanche war chiefs and in 1874 led a thousand Comanche, Kiowa, and Southern Cheyenne warriors against an outpost of buffalo hunters at Adobe Walls, a scant forty miles up the Canadian River from where I am writing this. It was to be the last flash of glory of a proud people, and it ended in failure. After the defeat of the Plains Indians in the Red River War of 1874–75, Quanah resigned himself to reservation life near Fort Sill, Oklahoma, took his mother's English name, and distinguished himself as a diplomat and leader of his people. He became a friend to Charles Goodnight, S. Burk Burnett, founder of the famed Four Sixes ranching empire, and even President Theodore Roosevelt, with whom he hunted wolves.

He also made the acquaintance of Billy Dixon, one of the buffalo hunters he had fought at the battle of Adobe Walls. Dixon recalled:

> "As we were riding along one day, [Quanah] began talking about the fight at the Walls. When I told him that I was one of the men that had fought against him, he leaned over on his horse and shook my hand. We became good friends." (Dixon 1927:136)

The story of Cynthia Ann Parker preserves in miniature the larger tragedy of her adopted people, like a seashell imitating the shape of a hurricane. It is impossible to read deeply in American frontier history without wincing at the way things turned out for the Comanches. Even the men who fought them, the Charles Goodnights and the Billy Dixons, admired their courage and, in old age, blinked back tears on seeing them reduced to wards of government. When the curtain fell at the end of Act

III, nobody but the most vociferous of the Indian-haters was cheering with much enthusiasm.

Those of us who have prospered at the expense of Quanah and his people are left to ponder about our success. I have done some of that; so have John Graves, Elmer Kelton, Larry McMurtry, Frederick Rathjen, and other modern writers who grew up in the region that used to be called the *comancheria*. Dan Flores was not a native son (his roots lay in East Texas and Louisiana) but he served for several years as an instructor at Texas Tech, and devoted an entire book to the ecology and history of the Llano Estacado. He viewed the imposition of European culture on the plains as a disaster that "substituted something soulless for something fine, wild, and free." He thunders:

> "The wild, pagan, sensuous men and women have been banished, the land de-buffaloed and de-wolved and de-grassed . . . [leaving] sorghum, wheat, and cotton fields, feedlots, swooping planes spraying poison across the landscape, vapor lamps, brick houses that look interchangeable. For this we wax lyrical over the pioneers?" (Flores 1990: 165)

Flores' book, which is beautifully written and handsomely illustrated with color photographs of the Caprock Canyonlands, gives expression to the dismay many of us have felt about "progress" that grinds away at open spaces and natural wonders, yet one balks at Flores' solution of turning the country back to the wolves and buffalo and a few Indian gardeners. There is something a little cracked about a discipline—professional ecology—that finds more value in mud huts and pumpkin-growing than in the accumulated wisdom of four thousand years of Western civilization. And it is always puzzling when professors embrace social models that would have no use for professors.

I am inclined to see history as an unending competition for resources, a cycle of ebb and flow that far exceeds our feeble attempts to assign it either good or evil. If rain falls, grass will grow and it will be eaten; if not by a buffalo then by a cow; if not by a cow then by a jackrabbit; if not by a jackrabbit then by a grasshopper.

The Comanches had their time and ruled the Llano for two hundred years, snatching it away from Apaches and Wichitas and Tonkawas and Caddos who had outlived, out-bred, out-fought, out-innovated, and outlasted unnamed Plains Village cultures (A.D. 1250-1450) who had erected their stone-slab houses over the pithouse ruins of Woodland people (A.D. 1-900), whose camp sites perched atop the litter left behind by the Archaic and Paleo peoples. No one can say what happened to those ancient folk, only that a wave washed over them and they disappeared.

My people, the Underhills, Shermans, Singers, and Currys, moved onto the plains as the Comanche wave receded. They came hungry for something—land, freedom, peace of mind, dignity, opportunity—and they wanted it more than the people they supplanted. Their story is not a morality tale but part of that mysterious drive, ultimately beyond our comprehension, that causes a sperm cell to seek out an egg, and a wounded animal to fight for its last gasps of air.

You can call that "greed" if you wish, but giving it a name explains nothing. More importantly, it changes nothing. Changing the course of history would be very expensive, and the activists who twitter about giving the Llano back to the Comanches aren't the ones who would pay the bill.

So we brood and fret. That is one of the things you can do when you're well-fed and have time on your hands.

Chapter Six: Loose Ends

In the summer of 1969 I drove down to Weatherford to see if I could locate Martha Sherman's grave. Grandmother Curry had told me that Sam Sherman, her nephew (the son of Forrest and Mary D Sherman), had located the grave several years before in a Weatherford cemetery. It had been unmarked, so he bought a gravestone and had it installed.

In Parker County, if you wanted to know about local history, you went to see Fred Cotten, the dean of Parker County historians. I found him in his place of business on Oak Street, across from the old stone courthouse. In this big limestone building, Mr. Cotten ran both a furniture store and a funeral home. An open door between the two establishments enabled him to wait on customers on both sides, although there weren't many customers the day I arrived. He was sitting in one of his display chairs in the furniture store, beneath a ceiling fan that stirred the humid air. He was up in years, probably in his seventies, and had a shock of fine white hair. He wore a wrinkled white shirt and baggy dress pants held up with suspenders, and a token necktie hung loose at his neck. I joined him under the fan and we talked about local history. I was surprised to learn that Mr. Cotten didn't number himself among those who admired Charles Goodnight. In fact, he had nothing good to say about him. In his wanderings through the Brazos River country, John Graves had encountered the same sentiment, and maybe from the same source:

"Old people around that country will tell you, with some bitterness, that Buenas Noches [Goodnight] had a big mouth and took credit for much that [Oliver] Loving did. It is so. But the Comanches got Oliver Loving on the Pecos . . . and Mr. Charlie lived to tell both their stories." (John Graves 1960: 62)

Fred Cotten was very familiar with the Martha Sherman story. In fact, he'd been so touched by it that, several years before, he had gone to the trouble of locating her grave and marking it with a stone, and had paid for it out of his own pocket. He also claimed to have saved the Willow Springs Cemetery from a Highway Department project that would have run a freeway right through the middle of it. When Mr. Cotten heard about the scheme, he threatened to take the matter to the courthouse and fight to the bitter end. I'll never know who actually paid for the small granite marker, Fred Cotten or Sam Sherman (Sam, I would bet), but I managed to locate the grave. The inscription said, "Martha Sherman. Killed by Indians in 1860. Buried at Willow Springs to be near a church." (Erickson 1995: 57-9)

What became of the Sherman Bible? Goodnight claims to have found it and says no more (Haley 1936:53), but in a letter written to the *Dallas Herald*, Sul Ross stated, "I found the Bible of Mrs. Sherman with her name on the flyleaf." (*Dallas Herald*, January 2, 1861) Uncle Roy Sherman told

Martha Sherman's grave in Willow Springs Cemetery, Weatherford, Texas. Photo courtesy Mike Harter and Barbara Whitton.

Edith Standhardt, "A leather covered Bible which had a leather shoulder strap on it was recovered, pierced halfway by a bullet. It is not known to whom the Bible belongs now." (Roy Sherman interview, 1963)

Mrs. Charles Haydon offered yet another version:

> "The Indians had with them the family Bible with an arrow hole about one third through the thickness. Ross brought back the Bible, also the scalp of Grandma, and the coat that was worn by the chief, which they said belonged to Mr. Sherman." (Haydon interview, 1965)

In Mrs. Haydon's version, Ross gave the items to Ezra Sherman, leaving us to wonder what a grieving man does with the scalp of his dead wife. In a loose file in the Texas Archives, a jumble of letters and notes from Parker and Tarrant Counties, I came across a newspaper story (no date or source listed) about Cynthia Ann and Quanah Parker. It reported that Sul Ross put several items from the Battle of Pease River on display in the state capitol and then donated them to Sam Houston. Mrs. Sherman's Bible might have been among those items. Apparently nobody knows what became of it, but it has left the family and is probably residing in a museum somewhere in Texas.

Another loose end in the Martha Sherman story concerns the presence among the Comanches of a warrior with red hair and green eyes. Most of the accounts don't mention it, including the version given by Charles Goodnight, whose memory in old age seemed above question. I first encountered the redhead in John Graves's version of the Sherman story in *Goodbye To A River*. This was a fictionalized retelling of the story and not a strict piece of scholarship, but there is no doubt in my mind that Mr. Graves had done his book-work and had come upon the redheaded man in some original source that he considered reliable. In the Graves episode, the "green-eyed, lean, redheaded Comanche" is the main villain, and the one who pierced Mrs. Sherman with a lance and scalped her. (John Graves 1960:137)

Since the other versions of the story didn't mention this redhead, I gave it no thought until a few years ago, when I ran across an article written by a man named Doyle Marshall, published in the *West Texas Historical Association Year Book.*

"During the four days in November, 1860, that she lived, after having been assaulted, scalped, and left naked by the Comanches on the prairie near the Parker-Palo Pinto county line, Mrs. Martha Sherman repeatedly and shamefully referred to her assaulter as 'that big old red-headed Indian.'" (Marshall 1985:88)

In a footnote, Marshall cited three sources for this information.

Marshall went on to say that historians have been puzzled by the mention of one or more red-haired men reported to have been seen with Indians on the frontier, and have wondered if they were white captives who, like Cynthia Ann Parker, had been absorbed into the tribe, or were they outlaws who found it profitable to work with the Indians?

"By provoking excitement about Indian hostilities, the outlaws were able to rob and plunder and shift the blame onto the Indians. . . . The Martha Sherman tragedy was not the first time that a red-haired Anglo had cooperated with the Indians in their savagery along the North Texas frontier." (Marshall 1985:89)

On September 29, 1872 Colonel Ranald S. Mackenzie and his Fourth Cavalry Regiment fought a battle with a band of Kotsoteka Comanches in the southeastern Texas Panhandle. One of the victims of that skirmish was a big red-haired man who had ridden with the Comanches. In writing of the incident later, Captain R. G. Carter, Mackenzie's adjutant, identified the red-head as Thomas F. M. McLean, an American who, incredibly, had once attended West Point. (Carter, *On the Border With Mackenzie*, as cited in Marshall 1985:96)

> "Because of his unruly shock of red hair, oversized features, general courseness, and ungainly manner, he was nicknamed 'Bison' or 'Bise.' Upon leaving [West Point] because of undesirable conduct, McLean drifted from place to place, but at each location was forced to move on because of his lawless character and unacceptable behavior. Reasoning that the life of a desperado in civilized society was becoming too hazardous, he fell in with and became a leader in a band of Comanches...After Mackenzie's battle with the Kotsotekas, the body of a renegade white man with a thick shock of red hair and fitting the singular description of 'Bise' McLean was found on the battlefield." (Marshall 1985:97)

Was Bise McLean the man who murdered Martha Sherman in 1860? Marshall considered him a likely suspect. I don't know what to think of these stories of the red-headed killer. The fact that it doesn't appear in any of the main sources, or in the Sherman-Curry accounts, makes me wonder about its accuracy. On the other hand, it is clear that John Graves and Doyle Marshall didn't invent the story out of thin air. John Graves didn't cite the sources of his information, but Marshall's piece is documented and gives every indication of being carefully researched.

The best we can say, perhaps, is that some of Martha Sherman's neighbors in Parker and Palo Pinto counties believed the story was true and passed it along to later generations. As Mr. Graves himself wrote, "The bag of fragmentary, jumbled, contradictory tales left over from the frontier is lumpy with mysteries like that, and no one will ever solve them now." (John Graves 1960:140)

There is also a series of coincidences that run through the Sherman episode, weaving an intriguing tapestry out of the lives of Martha Sherman and Cynthia Ann Parker. Both came from families that were bold enough to settle on the edge of the Texas frontier, both families moved to Texas from Illinois (coincidentally, so did Charlie Goodnight's family), and in 1860 Cynthia Ann and Martha were close to the same age. Both had dramatic, life-changing encounters with the Comanches, and in most accounts, Mrs. Sherman was killed by Cynthia Ann's husband, Peta Nocona. Both women suffered the death of a baby and both left sons who later appeared in West Texas—Joe Sherman and Quanah Parker.

Oddly, Martha Sherman was buried in *Parker* County which had been named in honor of Cynthia Ann's uncle Isaac, a member of the Third, Fourth, Sixth and Seventh Congresses of the Republic of Texas, and a member of the first State Constitutional Convention in Texas. Isaac Parker died in Weatherford and may even be buried in Willow Springs Cemetery, where Martha Sherman was laid to rest. (Fulmore 1915:88-9)

Odder still, Martha Sherman and Cynthia Ann Parker were actually related by marriage. Mrs. Charles Haydon, Martha's granddaughter, recalled, "Cynthia Ann Parker was a second cousin of my father on his father's side. The two families all lived in Illinois and moved to Texas along about the same time." (Haydon, newspaper article 1925)

A strange ending to a famous piece of Texas history.

Chapter Seven: J. Evetts Haley

In the fall of 1961 the Perryton Ranger football team played the Quanah Indians for the district championship. I was a proud member of that Ranger team, yet so ignorant of my region's history that I didn't notice the irony of this contest. My Rangers had taken their name from the legendary Texas Rangers and the town of Quanah had been named in honor of Quanah Parker. Our clash on the football field, in other words, became a symbolic reenactment of the Battle of Pease River, only with different results. In 1961 the Rangers lost and the Indians won.

When I was growing up in Perryton, J. Evetts Haley was one of the very few authors the Texas Panhandle had ever produced. In high school we were never exposed to his books on Fort Concho, the XIT ranch, George Littlefield, and Charles Goodnight, all first-rate works of scholarship about the very region we were occupying, the northwest Texas High Plains. When I graduated from high school in 1962, I'm not sure I would have even recognized Haley's name. Looking back, I see this as a sad omission, and it is no wonder that I marched off to college thinking that I had grown up in a cultural wasteland and that all writers lived in New York and Boston. In fact, the Panhandle had produced a small handful of authors in addition to Mr. Haley: Laura V. Hamner, Olive King Dixon, Luella Grace Ehrdman, John McCarty, and a reclusive novelist in Amarillo named Al Dewlin.

I had never heard of them, nor had I ever been exposed to Billy Dixon's fine autobiography, *The Life of Billy Dixon*, which he dictated to his wife Olive. Dixon's book appeared in 1914, followed by Haley's Goodnight book in 1936, which means that both had been around long enough to have percolated down into the curriculum of a small town school system in the fifties and sixties, yet they were not part of my educational experience. We slogged through *Tristam Shandy* and *Beowulf* but were never exposed to books that might have explained how and why people happened to occupy our little town and the other little towns we played against in football, or why our teams carried the names of Rangers, Kiowas, Comanches, and Bison. I discovered both books that evening in 1966 when Grandmother Curry went off to bed and I drifted into Buck Curry's library.

After my visit with Grandmother, I returned to Austin and bought a copy of the Goodnight book at the Garner and Smith Bookstore on Guadalupe Street. I devoured it in three sittings and found it utterly captivating, worthy of every bit of the praise it has received in the six decades since Haley wrote it. Not only did Mr. Haley do a thorough job of researching his subject, but his subject stood out in my mind as one of the great Americans of the nineteenth century. Every child in Texas, and especially in the Panhandle, should read the biography of this extraordinary man. More than just a frontiersman or cowboy, Goodnight possessed a first-rate mind and a photographic memory, was an original thinker, an amateur scientist, and an astute observer of everything he encountered in nature. John Graves said it well when he wrote, "[Goodnight] was a tough and bright and honorable man in tough not usually honorable times." (John Graves 1960: 62) You would have to say that the matching of Goodnight and J. Evetts Haley was one of the most fortuitous events in all of Texas literature.

In January of 1971 I was in Amarillo on some errand, and on impulse, decided to drive eighteen miles south to Canyon, where I knew Mr. Haley resided. I had thought of doing this several times before but had never worked up the courage. Mr. Haley had a reputation for being

A famous shot of Goodnight and buffalo bull. Photo courtesy Panhandle-Plains Historical Museum.

blunt, outspoken, opinionated, and explosive. No one could deny his credentials as a first-rate historian of the West, but during the fifties and sixties his involvement with political crusades had tarnished his reputation among scholars, including his one-time friend and colleague at the University of Texas, J. Frank Dobie.

During the early sixties, Haley and a group called Texans for America had led a vicious attack on historian Paul F. Boller, Jr., then a professor at Southern Methodist University, accusing him of being "soft on Communism." They dealt him much misery and succeeded in killing the sales of his high school textbook in Texas. (Boller 1992: 24ff)

I had taken an honors course under Dr. Boller while he was a visiting professor at the University of Texas in 1963–4 and I knew that the charges against him were fatuous. Boller was not only a fair and decent man, but also a meticulous scholar (Phi Beta Kappa and three degrees from Yale) and the best teacher I had in six years of university education—always stimulating, prepared, and demanding excellence from his students. After college, Paul Boller and I remained friends and he was a guest in our home many times. In 1967, he even served as a groomsman in my wedding.

How Mr. Haley could have been so right in his admiration of Charles Goodnight and so wrong in his evaluation of Paul Boller, I never understood. It revealed a side of him that I didn't comprehend or admire. I got the impression that at some point in his youth, Haley fell deeply in love with the nineteenth century and acquired a kind of loathing for his own times. After leaving a research position at the University of Texas, he seemed to have retreated into an angry exile in the Panhandle, where he severed all ties with the mainstream of Texas literature and culture. There, he ran cattle on his JH ranch, fumed about the sorry state of modern America, self-published his books, and sold them to a list of admirers who shared his interest in frontier history.

Part of my reluctance to meet him stemmed from the fact that I belonged to a generation for which he felt monumental contempt, and which had produced most of the social foment of the sixties. In 1971 I still wore a beard and a buzzard's nest of long curly hair, even though my wife, Kris, and I had moved back to Perryton the year before. I had a feeling that Mr. Haley wouldn't approve of my appearance, and he didn't. Did I dare present myself on his doorstep and ask for an audience, and would he talk to me? It would be risky, but we did have at least one point in common. I was the great-great grandson of Martha Sherman, and that was a name he would recognize and respect.

I drove to his attractive Spanish-style home on a quiet tree-lined street, just a few blocks from the campus of West Texas State University. I rang the doorbell and waited. After a bit, the door opened and I looked into the stern gaze of an attractive middle-aged woman who turned out to be Mr. Haley's second wife. (His first wife, Nita Stewart Haley, had died several years before). She swept me with her eyes and asked my name, my purpose in being there, and if I had an appointment with Mr.

Haley. I said that I was an aspiring author from Perryton, an admirer of Mr. Haley's historical books, and a descendant of Martha Sherman. She invited me inside, saying that she would have to see if Mr. Haley were available. She ushered me into the library and left me alone.

The room had a pleasant aroma of wood, books, and leather. A gas stove set into the south wall gave a friendly light to what was otherwise a rather dark room, expressive of twilight and solitude. A metal desk occupied the center of the room and upon it sat a typewriter, a dictating machine, and a rotary card file for names and addresses. Everything was neat and in its proper place. I glanced around the bookshelves that lined the walls and were filled with volumes that had been arranged in meticulous order. My eye caught the names of several authors: H. L. Mencken, J. Frank Dobie, De Toqueville, Andy Adams. There was a section on western outlaws and another devoted to Mr. Haley's own

J. Evetts Haley holding a big yearling on his rope, probably on his JH ranch south of Spearman, Texas. Haley's knowledge of range life didn't come entirely from his collection of books. Photo courtesy Panhandle-Plains Historical Museum.

considerable output, and files of research notes contained in large brown envelopes.

Other shelves held old spurs, a powderhorn, and branding irons. Saddle blankets covered the floor, providing some warmth against the January chill. The chairs were heavy and severe, made of sturdy wood and requiring the sitter to maintain an upright posture. I noticed several framed pieces of art on the west wall, one painting and three pencil drawings by Harold Bugbee, the Panhandle artist who had done the illustrations for Mr. Haley's Goodnight book. I had always admired Bugbee's drawings. He had a gift for recording the minutest details of horses and men at work, and for capturing the starkness of the plains. Like a great orator who understands the impact of pauses, Bugbee used blank space to express a landscape without trees or mountains. I moved closer and studied one of Bugbee's most famous drawings, the pencil sketch of Old Man Goodnight—that magnificent Olympian head with its down-turned mouth, gray beard, and smoldering eyes.

I heard footsteps on the stairs and a moment later Mr. Haley entered the room. He walked slowly and deliberately, stood about five-feet ten in his boots, and had a slender build. His hair was gray and thin, and his face had a reddish cast to it, with a nose that formed a slight bulb on the end. There was an air of dignity about him and he didn't seem much inclined to foolishness. His piercing gaze seemed harsh, almost angry, as he looked me over, but it began to soften as we sat down and talked. He had pretty eyes when he wasn't scowling. I gave him my Sherman credentials right away and asked if he knew what had become of Mrs. Sherman's Bible. He didn't. I told him about my ranching relatives in Gaines County. I knew that he had grown up in a ranching family around Midland and thought he might have crossed paths with some of the Shermans. He had not, but we found a common interest when I mentioned that all my kinfolks in Gaines County had known the famous outlaw, Tom Ross.

Mr. Haley warmed to that subject right away and was very familiar with one of the stories Mother had told me about Tom Ross, his murder of two cattle inspectors in the Gaines Hotel in Seminole. In fact, Mr. Haley had personally known Ross's accomplice in the killing, Milt Good ("He was a good calf roper") and one of the victims, H. L. Roberson ("An ambitious man who spread it around that he was going to get Tom Ross").

Then he said, "When Milt Good got out of prison, he wrote a book. Did you know that?" I didn't. "He published it himself and it's hard to find." This fascinated me. I had heard many stories about Ross and Good from Mother and my great-uncles, but I had never seen anything written about them. I made a note to myself: "Find Milt Good's book." I did find it . . . thirty-one years later.

I told Mr. Haley about the trip I had made to Weatherford to locate the grave of Martha Sherman, and of my conversation with old Fred Cotten: "He had nothing favorable to say about Charles Goodnight. I was surprised."

Mr. Haley snorted. "A lot of people didn't. A lot of people despise great men. Goodnight was a great man. There's a lot of jealousy down there about Goodnight."

During our conversation, which stretched into several hours, Mrs. Haley entered the room twice, then left without a word. I got the impression that she wanted to be sure that I wasn't up to some kind of mischief. But when she returned the third time, she seemed to have decided that I was all right, and asked if I could stay for lunch. I said I could. Mr. Haley took it upon himself to cook the meat, thick patties of lean ground sirloin. When we sat down at the table, he announced that he'd cooked the meat *rare*, by heaven, the way beef ought to be eaten, implying that anyone who didn't like rare beef was something less than a true Texan. He watched with hawk eyes to see how I would respond. It was my good fortune that I shared his taste for rare beef. I ate it, it was delicious, and he let me off the skewer of his gaze.

But I could see that something was still gnawing at his gizzard and finally he couldn't hold it back any longer. "John, you seem a pretty nice kid, but why do you wear those blankity-blank whiskers?"

I had expected this and had prepared my answer. "Mr. Haley, after reading your book, I admired Charles Goodnight so much, I wanted to grow a beard, just as he did." That was a small lie, but it stopped the interrogation. Old Haley stared at me for a moment, then grunted "huh" and poked a fork into his steak. I glanced at his wife and saw a flicker of a smile before she turned away. It appeared that I had survived my testing and had even amused the lady of the house.

In 1977, six years later, I was punching cows on a ranch in Beaver County, Oklahoma, and had begun writing articles for *Livestock Weekly*, Stanley Frank's fine paper published out of San Angelo. Every issue had an original cartoon by Ace Reid and the associate editor was a fellow named Elmer Kelton, who also happened to be a very accomplished writer of western novels. Every cowboy and rancher I knew read *Livestock Weekly*, and so did Mr. Haley. I received a letter from him in February.

> "I've been reading your column in the *Livestock Weekly* and wondering if you are the same character who showed up from behind a bushy beard at my home some years ago. Whether you are or whether you ain't (I suspect you are) I want to say that I'm enjoying your sketches and watching with interest the development and improvement of your style. . . . Keep up this sort of thing, and the weekly routine, deadline. Searching for and developing a subject cannot be beaten as schooling for a writer. Great discipline!" (Haley letter, February 17, 1977)

The following year he sent me another letter of encouragement. "I am glad to see that you are staying with the genuine stuff. You may starve but you will maintain your self respect." (Haley letter, April 13, 1978)

> I didn't see him again until June of 1983, when the Western Writers of America (WWA) held its annual convention in Amarillo. In my capacity as program chairman, I asked Mr. Haley to address the group. With some reluctance, he agreed

to do it. He came to the convention hotel with Mrs. Haley and Byron Price, who was then serving as director of the Panhandle-Plains Historical Museum in Canyon, a tall dashing young historian in cowboy boots and wearing a dark mustache. Mr. Haley was eighty-two but still vigorous and alert. He walked without a cane, even though he told our group that over his long life, he had sustained five broken legs, three broken collarbones, one broken jaw, and uncounted damaged ribs—from horse-related accidents, I assumed, not from political debates.

Before Mr. Haley made his address, Byron gave us a surprise that took my breath away. He had brought a short piece of grainy black and white film from the museum archives. It showed a young Evetts Haley, fresh out of graduate school, interviewing the Old Man himself. Bent but still defiant at the age of ninety-two, Goodnight moved about the room, throwing out his hands in bold gestures, his body still expressing energy and power. I could hardly believe it, but there on the screen was the man who had led Sul Ross's Rangers after the Comanches in 1860, the man who had found Martha Sherman's Bible in the mud. When Mr. Haley

Goodnight as he was captured by a movie camera. In a 1930 letter to Panhandle artist Harold Bugbee, Haley wrote: "Here are some enlargements made from motion picture film...Colonel [Goodnight] never knew when these were being made and consequently he is shown entirely oblivious to photography...These are the pictures of him laughing, and almost the only ones, I've ever seen." Letter and photograph from Goodnight file, Panhandle-Plains Historical Museum.

took the platform, he recalled his first meeting with Goodnight, when he dropped in unannounced at the old man's ranch house. Goodnight had been dictating letters to a stenographer when Haley knocked. Goodnight answered the door, scowling as only he could scowl, like Zeus awakened from a nap.

Young Haley said, "I'm sorry to bother you, Mr. Goodnight, but a friend suggested that I come and meet you."

"Don't worry about it," Goodnight snarled. "If you hadn't come, some other SOB would have."

I found that story especially amusing, since it brought back parallel memories of my first meeting with Mr. Haley.

In his address to the WWA, Haley took aim at modern writers who dismiss the cowboy as a "myth" and try to diminish the importance of the frontier experience. He spoke of nature as "the great purifier" and praised the simple honesty of cowboy prose. He talked about the old pioneers he had met and read passages from his books. Several times his voice choked with emotion. Mr. Haley seemed to have mellowed with age. When he finished his speech, the crowd of two hundred writers and editors rose to their feet and gave him a standing ovation. I was standing beside Mrs. Haley, both of us applauding. She leaned toward me and whispered that it was the best presentation she had ever heard him give.

Later that day, when Mr. Haley and I had a moment alone, I asked him if he'd ever met another man who compared to Charles Goodnight. "No, never. He was unique. He was a great man."

Chapter Eight: John Graves

I remember sitting on an airplane and watching the man across the aisle from me. He had oriental features and was reading a newspaper covered with Chinese characters that had no more meaning to me than chicken tracks. Yet those marks on the page caused him to smile and frown, and held his attention during a flight that lasted two hours. This left me thinking about the wonder of written language and the miracle that occurs when the human mind transforms those lines of type into mental pictures. Printed words can cause us to laugh, cry, think, remember, and shake with anger. They can alter our blood pressure, dilate the pupils of our eyes, raise the hair on the back of our necks, and cause our breath to quicken. Books have started wars, brought down tyrants, altered history, and caused people to fall in love.

Words have a power that is almost mystical, and our ability to transform scribbles on the page into feelings and actions is one of the spiritual qualities that sets us apart from our dogs and cats, and defines us as humans. Sometimes the direction of a person's life can be changed by what he reads in a book. I can point to several books that have had a profound effect on me. Stories from the Old Testament gave me the heroes of my boyhood. When Mrs. Smith, my fourth grade teacher, read *Tom Sawyer* aloud to our class, it hit with the force of revelation that reading need not be a joyless experience, that a gifted writer can trap the sounds and nuances of the spoken word like butterflies and turn them loose to fly out of a page of printed type.

Mr. Haley's biography of Goodnight opened a door on my Texas roots, and John Graves's *Goodbye to a River* gave me a template for combining the love of words with an affection for one's soil. I don't know if my life would have turned out differently if I had never read *Goodbye to a River*, but it might have. I think my cousin Mike Harter was the first to call my attention to it, and Kris gave me a copy of it for Christmas in 1969. It made a huge and lasting impression. Here was an author who wrote on subjects that were often shrugged off as "regional," yet he wrote about them with such precision and wisdom that his sentences resonated in my imagination. His slow, careful stalking of the truth might begin with observations about a horsefly or a Spanish goat, but somehow it turned one's thoughts toward the stars, and beyond. Texas novelist Marshall Terry has described Graves as "a stylistically elegant writer" and "a whole human being . . . . He is who he is but there is just a slight ironic edge to him that, mostly playfully, warns you against taking too seriously what an 'old crock' (his term) like himself might utter." (Clifford and Pilkington 1989: 143)

I met John Graves just as I had met Mr. Haley, showing up unannounced and uninvited—a practice I have come to disavow, now that I am an aging man of Texas Letters myself. But in those days, I was on a mission and had no shame. It was in the fall of 1973 and I had driven down to Austin to meet with Bill Wittliff. Today, Wittliff is best known as the author of the screenplay for "Lonesome Dove," but in 1973 he was building a reputation as a photographer and owner of a small publishing company called Encino Press. He had read my *Through Time and the Valley* in manuscript and wanted to publish it through Encino Press. That didn't work out and the book was published five years later by Shoal Creek Publishers, but at the time I was elated. I felt that, at last, I had become a real author.

The book described a fifteen-day horseback trip I made down the Canadian River valley in 1972, and I explained to Bill that I had gotten my idea for the book's structure after reading *Goodbye To A River*. Bill didn't seem surprised. Books that imitated John Graves had almost become a separate category in Texas literature, as Graves was without question the writer most admired by other Texas writers. We all wanted to imitate his precise, methodical style of writing and few ever succeeded. Bill asked if I had met John Graves. No. Did I want to? Of course. "On your way back to the Panhandle, stop by Glen Rose and visit with him. Tell him I suggested it."

Around two on the afternoon of October 7, I drove into the little town of Glen Rose, south of Fort Worth, got Mr. Graves's phone number out of the directory, and called him from a pay phone. After several rings, he answered. As rapidly as possible, I explained that I had read and admired his work, that Bill Wittliff had suggested I drop by for a visit, and that I was the great-great grandson of Martha Sherman, whose story he had recounted in *Goodbye To A River*. I held my breath and

John Graves at Hardscrabble in the early 1970s. Photo courtesy of the Southwestern Writers Collection, Texas State University.

waited through a moment of silence. "Well, come on out. I'm not doing anything special." He gave me directions to his place outside of town, which he called Hard Scrabble. I found my way with no trouble, but the rocky road to his house almost destroyed my little Ford Pinto.

When I pulled up to the house, a man wearing khaki pants, a faded blue denim work shirt, and a railroader's cap came out of the barn and walked toward me. I was surprised that a man who looked so ordinary had written a book as fine as *Goodbye To A River*. He resembled the men you might see in a small town café at lunchtime—welders, farmers, mechanics, carpenters, bricklayers. He wasn't what I had expected, this man who held degrees from Rice and Columbia. We shook hands and I followed him to the house. He fixed us glasses of iced tea and we sat on the screened porch, groping for conversation that would justify my invasion of his sanctuary. It came slowly at first. John Graves was no chatterbox, but Mrs. Sherman's story gave us some common ground and then we moved into subjects that seemed to interest him more: his bees, goats, and cattle, and his various projects to restore native grasses on his four hundred acres of rock and cedar.

Then we moved down to his study, a small room in the northwest corner of the barn. There was a wooden desk against the north wall, holding an ancient manual typewriter and heaps of letters, bills, and scribbled notes. He apologized for the mess and said he was going to straighten things up one of these days. He sat in a chair at the desk and used a big brass spittoon on the floor beside him. By this time, we had warmed to each other and we talked through the entire afternoon, covering a wide range of subjects: books, authors, Texas history, coyotes, birds, carpentry, farm machinery, hay, poetry, dogs, family history, the seasons of the year, religion, guns, and writing. Without the slightest hint of pretension, he made references to Milton, Shakespeare, Joyce, Hemingway, Faulkner, Jung, Freud, Dobie, O'Henry, Dos Passos, Mailer, and Bellow. It appeared to me that he had not been much influenced by Texas literature.

"I like most Texas writers, but if you want to know whom I admire, I would say only Katherine Anne Porter. She spent her life trying to prove she wasn't from Texas, but her early works were set in Texas and those were her best."

He said his writing style had been most influenced by O'Henry— "Although I hate to admit it"—and James Joyce. He lamented that he was not a very disciplined writer and hadn't produced much. I pointed out that anyone who had written *Goodbye To A River* didn't need to write much else. He smiled and said that he did his writing in snatches. Sometimes he'd wake up in the night with a complete passage in mind, jot it down and go back to it later. He preferred to do his writing in the morning and to do physical labor the rest of the day. He showed me some black and white photographs that Bill Wittliff had taken of him. There were three of them and I noticed that each appeared to show a different man: a university professor, a Southern laborer, and a Texas rancher. And stranger still, the John Graves I was looking at in person didn't show much resemblance to any of them. How did he explain that? "I've always been lucky that I don't have a face people remember," he said. "If I look like four different people, maybe I am."

Around dark, Jane Graves, John's wife, drove in from town with her two daughters, Sally and Helen. She was a kind lady and seemed glad to meet me. She told us to come up to the house for a drink and some supper, and we moved back to the house. After supper, we drifted back out to the screen porch and resumed our conversation deep into the night. At one point Mr. Graves stopped talking and cocked his ear. "That's a screech owl . . . no, two of them. Before the night's over, they'll be up around the house." Later, he heard the baying of a hound in the distance. "That's Kenneth's dog. They're running foxes tonight."

Shameless to the end, I hung around until midnight, and by then it was too late to start driving back to the Panhandle. Mr. Graves was kind enough to invite me to stay the night (what else could he do?), and I made a bed on the couch. When I left the next morning, I got the feeling that he had enjoyed our visit, but also that he would be relieved to get back to his bees and goats. After that, we kept in touch through letters. I had gone to cowboying and was collecting rejection slips from New York publishers. I wrote him sprawling four-page letters filled with souped-up, over-heated prose, letters I saved as carbon copies and now find embarrassing. He wrote back one- and two-page gems of precision-built sentences, hacked out on his manual typewriter in the barn.

"I am glad if our day together meant something to you; I found it pleasant also. I am, as you will have discerned, not a very august type and probably the best of what I am and whatever I know has gone and will go into my writing. But occasionally one hits upon a younger friend who is enough like himself— in background and in thrust and perception—that some communication is possible, some illusion of being able to pass along relevant observations. It is a good feeling." (John Graves letter, March 30, 1974)

In my letters I expounded on theories of writing, whole mountains of them, and he wrote back his quiet, sensible advice:

"I still believe that the best writing pulls in one way or another toward spoken language and the old short hard powerful Anglo-Saxon vocabulary. But like most rules this one was made to be broken when you learn enough to be able to break it right, and it is always necessary to take into account people like, say, John Milton, to whom it would have been repugnant nonsense from the start. I know that for me at least to be able to maintain a sense of spoken language in writing is absolutely necessary, like Antaeus touching the earth, but I feel best about my writing when it is going sort of on tiptoes, touching earth but not rolling on it." (John Graves letter, September 14, 1974)

And again in 1976:

"If I and my work have meant something to you, that is very pleasant and I appreciate your generosity in saying so. Influence from other writers works on us all, of course; it is part of the continuity of language and literature." (John Graves letter, November 6, 1976)

Recently, browsing through my file of John Graves letters, I came across a short handwritten message he sent in 1979: "The cowdog piece was really fine. Keep it up. Regards, hastily, John G." (John Graves letter, August 7, 1979)

I don't know to what piece of writing he was referring, probably something I had published in *Livestock Weekly* or *The Cattleman*. It must have been one of my earliest efforts to write in the voice of *Hank the Cowdog*. The first book in that series didn't appear until four years later.

I can't excuse the impertinence I showed in meeting J. Evetts Haley and John Graves, but I have treasured the time I spent in their company. Both are writers I admire and both of them helped to steer me back to my Texas roots . . . back to the stories my mother told me about the Shermans.

Chapter Nine: Joe Sherman

History has cast a bright light on Cynthia Ann Parker and Martha Sherman, but has had very little to say about the two-year old boy who stood in the rain that horrible day in November 1860, watching as his father tied a rag around the scalped head of his dying mother.

Joe Sherman seems to have been a shadowy figure from the very beginning, a man who moved through life like a coyote, casting backward glances to see if he was being followed. Though he qualified as a genuine Texas frontiersman and pioneer, he made no effort to record his adventures and seemed content to take his past with him to the grave, leaving it to others to write the history books and figure out who he was, if that's what they wanted to do. If he ever bothered to write a memoir, my branch of the family never saw evidence of such. It has taken me forty years to assemble a hazy pattern of where he was and what he did—family stories, bits of stories, county records, newspaper files, and a reference here and there in a book. And I'm sure that's the way he wanted it. My cousin Mike Harter, a historian by training, helped fill in some of the blank spaces, based on his memory of conversations with his mother and other family members:

"After Martha's death, Joe was sent to live with her mother in Limestone County. She doted on him as she grieved for her daughter, and mothered him until she died when he was about seven. Her death must have been a big shock to young Joe. He was sent to live with Martha's brother, Jeremiah Johnson, the family patriarch of the Hawkins clan. He was something of a tyrant and I'm under the impression that Joe Sherman hated him, or hated being a slave on his farm. At the age of thirteen, Joe took off with some outlaws. That is believable to me because it would have been about 1871. Reconstruction was in full bloom. E. J. Davis was governor and lawlessness was abroad in the land. I'm under the impression that he roamed with them for a while but left them after something really bad happened. He returned to the countryside west of Fort Worth, where Jim Loving took him under his wing." (Harter letter, July 13, 2004)

No one in the family seems to know exactly what kind of trouble Joe Sherman got into. Mother said only that if he hadn't married a strong Quaker woman, he might have become an outlaw. It might have had something to do with gathering unbranded cattle, a common though shady practice after the Civil War, or it might have been something more serious. An 1891 letter to Joe Sherman from his aunt Sarrah Clinesmith (Martha Sherman's sister) hints that she may have known something of his past:

> "Dear boy, have you quit being wicked? Are you trying to live a Christian [life] so when you leave your friends on earth, you will meet those dear friends you have in heaven? Your poor mother, killed by the cruel savage, said she wanted you all raised in the love and fear of the Lord so you would meet her in heaven." (Clinesmith letter, 1891)

Sometime around 1871 or 1872, Joe Sherman returned to Palo Pinto County and came under the good influence of one of the pioneering families in the area, the Lovings. Palo Pinto County seems to have been an incubator for famous Texas cattlemen and included the names

Charles Goodnight; George Slaughter and his illustrious sons, John, W. B., and C. C. Slaughter; and the Loving clan—Oliver and his sons, James C., Bill, George, and Joseph—all of whom carved their names deeply into the tree of frontier history. It also produced a large crowd of lesser known cowboys and ranchers who would eventually make their way west to Crosby County, Joe Sherman among them. A Texas historical marker in Palo Pinto County states that Oliver Loving was the first trail driver of Texas cattle. (Palo Pinto Historical Commission, 1986: 379) When I first encountered this claim, I was skeptical about it, as I had supposed that old Shanghai Pierce down on the Texas coast had been the first of the Texas trail drivers.

An imposing man of six-feet-six, with a voice like a foghorn, whose last will and testament required that he be buried standing up in his grave, Pierce swam his cattle across wide muddy rivers all the way to New Orleans, and he was doing it during the Civil War, before the Trail Driving Period actually began around 1866. (Emmett, 1953) But no less an authority than Goodnight confirmed that Oliver Loving was trailing herds before the war:

> "I positively know [that] the first herd driven north out of northwest Texas was driven in 1858 by Oliver Loving, leaving Palo Pinto and Jack counties, thence north to . . . the Arkansas River, to just above where Pueblo [Colorado] now stands." (Hunter and Saunders 1925: 952)

Oliver Loving and Goodnight established a partnership in 1866, when Loving was fifty-four and Goodnight thirty, and drove herds of cattle from Palo Pinto County to Fort Sumner, New Mexico. The following year, Loving sustained serious wounds in a skirmish with Indians and died in Fort Sumner. Before he died, he begged Goodnight to transport his body back to Texas, as he did not want to be buried in a "foreign land." Goodnight was a man of his word. Several months later, he and Joe Loving returned to Fort Sumner, exhumed the body, loaded it upon a wagon, and began what J. Evetts Haley described as "the strangest and most touching funeral cavalcade in the history of the cow country" (Haley 1936:184), the six hundred mile trip across the Trans Pecos desert and back to Palo Pinto County. In the movie version of *Lonesome Dove*, Tommy Lee Jones recreated this episode with an unforgettable performance.

Mother told me that after running away from home, Joe Sherman went to work for "the Lovings," omitting once again crucial details such as when, where, and which Lovings. My best guess is that he worked for J. C. "Jim" Loving on the 32,000 acre Lost Valley ranch in Jack County. Jim Loving was the oldest of Oliver's four sons and the executor of his estate. In 1877 he met in Graham, Texas, with other prominent ranchers (including C. C. Slaughter, Burk Burnett, and Charles Goodnight) and founded the Stock Raisers Association of Northwestern Texas, which later evolved into today's Texas and Southwest Cattle Raisers Association. Loving served as the first secretary of the organization and later served as its general manger, and was affiliated with the association until his death in 1902. (Fairley newspaper article, 1999)

It was in the company of Jim Loving and his cowboys that Joe Sherman grew to manhood and learned the cowboy trade. Mother said that the Lovings were fond of him and that the cowboys became his family. In the small collection of Sherman memorabilia that has come down to us, there is an old newspaper clipping bearing the date 1904. It contains a story written by a man named R. S. Purdy of Cement, Oklahoma, telling of a skirmish between a group of Loving cowboys and some hostile Indians in July of 1874. A cowboy named John Heath was shot in the forehead and died in the battle. The fact that the Shermans kept this clipping (they were prone to use letters and personal papers as kindling) suggests that Joe Sherman might have been involved.

Mother said that one cold winter night, Joe was sleeping on the ground near the Loving chuck wagon. A big log rolled out of the fire and onto his legs, giving him a severe burn. For weeks he couldn't work and had to keep to his bed in the wagon, and it was then that he began reading Shakespeare. Mother said he loved and read Shakespeare throughout his life and kept a volume of the plays beside his bed until the day he died. Joe Sherman's passion for The Bard always puzzled me. In college, I trudged through enough Shakespeare to know that it isn't easy reading, and I wondered why a young cowboy, reading by the light of a campfire, would choose such difficult material. The answer comes from a man named John Preston Alley, an early pioneer on the South Plains and a long-time employee of Colonel C. C. Slaughter:

> "Since newspapers and magazines were not available, cowboys often read Shakespeare and other classics. . . . It was more the rule than the exception for the cowboy to read high class literature. I have many times seen the boys reading Shakespeare and other such literature." (Hill and Jacobs 1986: 43; Alley article, 1932: Part Five)

There is reason to suppose that John Alley and Joe Sherman knew each other, and Alley might have even had Sherman in mind when he made this observation. Before moving west onto the Staked Plains, Alley lived in Palo Pinto County where Joe Sherman spent much of his early manhood, and both men later made their way out to Crosby County. The 1880 census of Crosby County listed Alley as a cattleman located on Duck Creek. (Spikes and Ellis 1952: 26) We don't know exactly where Joe Sherman resided in 1880, but he probably wasn't far away.

While he was attached to the Loving family, Joe went on at least one trail drive up the Western Trail to Dodge City and Ogallala, Nebraska. Uncle Roy Sherman told me that his father mentioned being at Doan's Crossing on the Red River, and at Fort Sill, where Quanah Parker was living in peace with the white man. Uncle Roy also said that Joe Sherman knew Charles Goodnight quite well and always spoke highly of him. (Roy Sherman interview, 1971)

Joe lived for a year or so outside of Ogallala, then made his way back to Texas and joined what appears to have been a regular flood of cowpunchers who moved from Parker, Jack, and Palo Pinto Counties, out to the free grass ranges of the Llano Estacado. It was a good time to be making a start in the cattle business. "An abundance of free grass and increasing cattle prices caused a rush for West Texas lands. . . . Prices of grass-fed Texas steers rose from three dollars and fifty cents in 1878 to six dollars and fifty cents in 1882." (Jenkins 1986: 19)

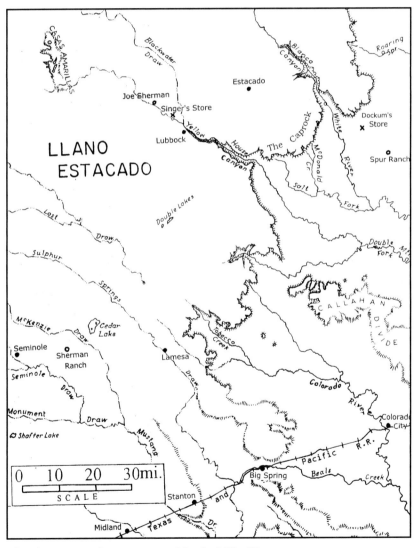

The Llano Estacado, 1880–1905. Map by Mike Harter.

Among the names that appear at the very beginning of High Plains history are men Joe Sherman certainly knew in Jack and Palo Pinto Counties: John, Will, and C. C. Slaughter; Will Sanders, Van Sanders, John Hensley, George Wolfforth, Sam Gholson, Rollie Burns, Felix Franklin, and John Alley; and up north in Palo Duro Canyon, Charlie Goodnight presided over the sprawling JA ranch. (Holden 1932: 90; W. Hubert Curry 1979: 180; Jenkins 1986: 19)

In 1883 we find Joe Sherman located on a ranch on McDonald Creek and Salt Fork of the Brazos in Crosby County (Spikes and Ellis 1952: 301; Claude Hall 1947; W. Hubert Curry 1979: 180), where he apparently lived with four other men: George Wolfforth, Bill Sanders, Van Sanders, and John Hensley. They might have been working as cowboys for one of the Slaughter outfits or for the 22 ranch. "John and Charles Hensley…had drifted their cattle from Jack County to the head of McDonald Creek in Crosby County in 1879. Their ranch was known as the 22 outfit." Rollie Burns worked for the Hensleys when he moved to the Llano in 1881. (Holden 1932: 72)

Max Coleman says that Sherman worked for a time with Nave-McCord Cattle Company on their Square and Compass Ranch in Garza County (near present-day Post), though it is not clear when that might have been or how long he stayed. (Coleman 1952: 138) While on the Square and Compass, he might have crossed paths with the colorful Rollie Burns, whose observations on frontier life were recorded by Professor W. C. Holden of Texas Tech University. Burns, who had worked for the Loving family in Jack County during the 1870s, managed the Square and Compass from 1884 and 1888.

> "Abram Nave and James McCord were wholesale grocers at Saint Jo, Missouri. . . . When cattle prices began to soar during the early 80's, they decided to invest their surplus in the cattle ranching business. In 1882 they bought 1500 head of cattle . . . and more cattle from George B. Loving in Jack County." (Holden 1932: 135)

Mrs. Charles Haydon said that Joe Sherman worked for Col. C.C. Slaughter, part of the time near Roswell, New Mexico.

> "When Mr. Slaughter was dividing up his property among his sons, he gave Joe Sherman part of the cattle, for he was regarded as one of the family. This gave Joe a beginning in the cattle business." (Haydon interview, 1965)

County records show that in 1887 the partnership of Franklin and Sherman registered the M-Cross brand in Crosby County. In October of 1889, Joe Sherman registered the brand in his own name. (Spikes and Ellis 1952:146) More than a century later, when I acquired my own ranch, I adopted the M-Cross as my brand in Roberts County, Texas.

In 1886, when residents of Crosby County took steps to form a county government, Estacado won the vote as county seat and a slate of candidates stood before the citizens for election in November. Some were Quakers and some were Gentiles, and nobody knew "how the Quaker support would go, as [the Quakers] expressed no love for the cattlemen" and "held all cattlemen at arm's length." (Spikes and Ellis 1952:19)

The Quakers had heard plenty of stories about rowdy young cowpunchers who drank whiskey, gambled, and brawled, and these were not qualities they wished to encourage in their Eden on the Prairie. John Cooper Jenkins notes that "this frontier Quaker village did not have the usual places of vice found in other frontier towns, such as gambling houses, dance halls, saloons, and houses of prostitution. Instead, there were churches, schools, literary societies, and a library. (Jenkins 1986: 149) Rollie Burns seemed to have gotten along well with the Quakers: "A lot of people [i.e., cowpunchers] thought they were queer, and wouldn't have anything to do with them; but that was because they never did get acquainted. All the Quakers I knew were splendid citizens." (Holden 1932: 187)

Apparently Joe Sherman won the trust of the Quakers. He was one of four county commissioners who won election, serving on a slate of officers that included Paris Cox as county clerk and Felix Franklin as sheriff. While staying in Harvey Underhill's hotel in Estacado, Joe took notice of the Underhills' daughter, Perlina, one of those pretty Quaker girls who turned the heads of the Gentile cowboys. The following passage comes from an unpublished manuscript about a surveyor named W. D. Twichell who, in 1886, was on a horseback trip in Crosby County. We can imagine that Joe Sherman might have been among the group of cowboys he observed, riding toward Estacado:

> "Twichell wondered why the cowboys were going to Estacado on Sunday. When they came to a rise overlooking the town he understood, for there was a 'beautiful bouquet:' the Quaker girls, dressed in all colors of calico, were walking to church. Twichell rode on into town. He stopped at a large frame house, the hotel which was operated by a Mr. Underhill." (Gracy manuscript, no date: 8)

According to my mother, one day Anna Underhill gave her daughter a secret smile and whispered, "Lina, I have found just the man for thee!" This would suggest that the Underhills approved of the young cowpuncher. Joe Sherman's cousin-by-marriage, Charles Singer, didn't remember it exactly that way:

> "Lina married that cowboy [Joe Sherman] and her folks raised the devil about that. They throwed a terrible fit. He was a pretty wild cowboy, deputy sheriff. He was one of the fastest men with a gun there was around there." (Charles Singer interview, 1982)

We have a letter written by Joe Sherman on April 9, 1887, saved by my distant relatives in the Hawkins family. He used two sheets of county letterhead paper ("The Office of the County Court, Crosby County") and wrote in a neat, firm hand, with some misspellings and little regard for the rules of capitalization:

Joe Sherman's letter to his aunt, written on Crosby County letterhead. Photo courtesy Barbara Whitton.

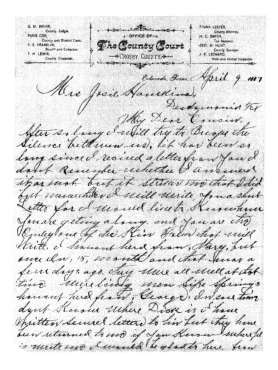

Mrs. Josie Hawkins:

Desdemona, Tex

My Dear Cousin:

After so long I will try to break the silence between us. It has been so long since I received a letter from you I don't remember whether I answered it or not. But it strikes me that I did but nevertheless I will write you a short letter for I would like to know how you are getting along and you are the only one of the kinfolks that will write. I haven't heard from Mary but once in fifteen months and that was a few days ago. They were all well at that time. We're living near Sipe Springs. Haven't heard from George in some time. Don't know where Dick is. I have written several letters to him but they have been returned to me. If you know where he is, write me. I would be glad to hear from him.

Well Josie most all of the people here are Quakers and all from the North. Myself and partner have built ourselves a good house here. It cost us twelve hundred dollars. It is very nice. Have three rooms and is painted inside and out. My partner [Felix Franklin] has just married and brought his wife here. She is very nice. She was raised at Weatherford. So you can guess how I am doing. My partner is sheriff of this Crosby County and we have got four hundred head of cattle and several horses.

Well, Josie, I must tell that I am going to get married next fall. My girl lives in this place [Estacado]. She is twenty years old. So I have written all I can think of. I will close with best wishes for your welfare. Give my kindest regards to all your folks.

P.S. Is Ben living with you yet? Tell him to write to me. Has he married yet? Suppose some of your own boys are big enough to work for you by this time. I must close by asking you to write to me soon and often. Address your letters to Estacado, Crosby County, Texas. Yours most respectfully,

Joe. Sherman

Sherman's repeated desire to communicate with his relatives suggests that even though he had left them behind, he felt a need to maintain some family ties, a theme that will appear later in his story. Also, the fact that he is partnered with Felix Franklin, the first sheriff of Crosby County (1886), shows that he had become a sober and upright citizen. Franklin, "a dashing young cowboy," won votes from the Quakers by promising that, if elected, he would support a ban on the sale of liquor in the county. (Spikes and Ellis 1951: 19)

Joe and Lina Sherman
shortly after their marriage
in Estacado. Photo courtesy
Martha Marmaduke and
Barbara Whitton.

The yoking of a pious Quaker girl with Joe Sherman, a tall hard-eyed cattleman, seems a bit strange. The Quakers abhorred violence. Joe Sherman had a long history of it, both before he met Lina Underhill and afterward. The Quakers placed a high value on education, yet Joe Sherman couldn't have had more than a few years of formal schooling. But something in Joe's nature must have pleased Lina's parents. Maybe he won them over by reciting Shakespeare. Or maybe, as Charles Singer remembered it, "they throwed a terrible fit," but to no avail. Lina and Joe were married in a Quaker ceremony December 29, 1887, with Reverend Anson Cox presiding, (Spikes and Ellis 1952: 204) and in November of the following year, the Shermans welcomed the first of their seven children into the world—my grandmother, Mable Clair Sherman, born in Estacado in November of 1888.

During the years 1885–7 Crosby County endured what historian W. C. Holden has called "the most disastrous drouth West Texas has ever experienced. For twenty-seven months there was not enough rain to settle the dust." (Holden, in Lawrence L. Graves 1962: 41) To make matters worse for ranchers, a severe blizzard in 1887 wiped out a huge number of cattle and the cattle market took a dizzying tumble. To supplement his ranching income, Joe took a job as deputy sheriff in a jurisdiction that included the sparsely populated counties of Crosby, Lubbock, Dickens, and Floyd. Billy Standifer had just been elected sheriff, replacing Sherman's business partner, Felix Franklin.

One day in 1889, a man named Dick Ware was sitting in the company store of the Spur Ranch on Duck Creek in Dickens County (Dockum's Store, it was called), the only such establishment for miles around. Suddenly, two transient cowboys named John Harvey and George Spencer burst in with pistols and yelled, "Hands up!" Since crime was almost unknown in this empty country, Dick Ware thought they were joking. They weren't. They tied Ware into his chair and covered his head with a gunny sack, then helped themselves to a small amount of cash, forty-two dollars' worth of postage stamps, and all the groceries they

Crosby County courthouse in Estacado, where Joe Sherman shot John Harvey. Photo courtesy Crosby County Pioneer Memorial Museum.

could carry. Leaving the store, they stole two Spur Ranch horses, a crime that was considered unforgivable on the frontier.

Deputy Joe Sherman rode after them, accompanied by a buffalo hunter named Sam Gholson, a Spur ranch employee named Harry Brown, and the storekeeper who had been robbed, Dick Ware. "They trailed the robbers with the sureness and tenacity of Apache Indians and captured them in a deep draw of the Yellow House Canyon." (Coleman 1931: 141)

Among the items Harvey and Spencer had stolen from the store were some dime novels.

"The desperados' weakness for literature proved their undoing. While they were resting under some trees in Yellow House Canyon, reading the dime novels, the posse overtook and quietly surrounded them. So absorbed were they in the stories, that an array of six shooter and Winchester barrels were pointing at them from every direction before they were aware of any intrusion." (Holden 1970: 207)

The prisoners were taken to Estacado, and the justice of the peace, Rev. George M. Hunt, conducted a hearing.

"After the evidence was all in, the lawyers became enraged and finally came to blows, using chairs for weapons. John Harvey, in attempting to dodge the lawyers, hobbled to the head of the stairs just as Joe Sherman, hearing the racket, started up from the sheriff's office with a rifle in his hand. Thinking Harvey was escaping, Sherman shot him through the right breast. Luckily, no bones were shattered, and the Justice of the Peace, who was just behind Harvey, was not struck. Harvey fell to the floor, turned deathly pale, and for a while pandemonium in general ruled. Things were finally quieted however, and the prisoners were held for trial." (Coleman article, 1931:141-2; also Holden 1970: 207, and Elliot 1939: 54)

In a little book of memoirs published in 1919, George Hunt, the justice of the peace, recalled, "I thought for awhile that Harvey's wound would prove fatal, but he soon revived. Doctor Marshburn was called, and extracted the bullet. The prisoner was taken to the jail, where he was nursed for several weeks, while he was recuperating." Hunt then adds this interesting detail. "The man who did the shooting pleaded guilty and waived his right to a preliminary hearing. He was released to await the action of the grand jury." (George Hunt 1919: 34)

That man would have been Joe Sherman, and I have found no record of the grand jury's verdict. Charles Singer said that Sherman was no-billed (Charles Singer interview, 1981), but he might have lost his job as deputy sheriff and the incident might have contributed to his decision the following year to move to Lubbock County. The publicity couldn't have pleased his Quaker in-laws.

The prisoners were later tried and convicted in Judge J. V. Cockerell's judicial district court and received sentences of eleven years in prison, with four years tacked onto Harvey's sentence "to ease the outraged feelings of Dick Ware." (Coleman 1931:142) They served their time in a federal penitentiary in Stillwell, Minnesota. W.J. Elliot said that Harvey died in prison, shot by a guard when he attempted to escape. (Elliot 1939: 59)

I don't think my mother ever knew this story about Joe Sherman, or at least she never mentioned it. I happened upon it in a small county library in Crosbyton, Texas. The author of the piece was a Lubbock rancher and attorney named Max Coleman, and I feel certain that he heard it straight from the mouth of Joe Sherman.

How, I wondered, did Mr. Coleman manage to pry the story out of the taciturn, tight-lipped frontiersman who had such an aversion to sharing his past? They must have been close friends and Sherman must have trusted him a great deal. Joe Sherman's widow, Lina Sherman, didn't share that feeling. When Coleman asked for her help in doing his research, she didn't answer his letters—a typical Sherman response to anyone who asked too many questions. (Bennett Kerr interview, 2004)

Joe Sherman probably never dreamed that his friend would eventually write the story down and get it published. But fourteen years after Sherman's death, Coleman did get it published in *Frontier Times* and managed to preserve it for future generations of Joe Sherman's curious relatives.

That wasn't the last piece of writing Max Coleman did on Joe Sherman. In 1952 he self-published a thin volume of memoirs about his early days on the Llano Estacado. It's a fine little book, but I doubt that it was known outside of a small circle of Coleman's family and close friends. I happened to find a copy of it in Buck Curry's library—with a penciled checkmark in the margin.

Coleman devotes an entire chapter to Joe Sherman and gives us the most comprehensive description ever recorded about this man of the shadows.

Chapter Ten: Max Coleman Remembers

In 1890 the Sherman family, which now included two children, Mable and Forrest, pulled up stakes and moved thirty miles west of Estacado to a ranch in Lubbock County. Mike Harter notes that "the Sherman ranch was located on Yellow House Draw where the town of Shallowater is currently situated. Grandmother Curry could remember that water flowed in Yellow House Draw. Today it is a sandy bed that has been plowed in many places." (Harter letter, July 13, 2004)

W. C. Holden says that until the 1920s there was a lake in Yellow House Canyon that covered about ten acres and was fed by springs on the west side. "The overflow from the lake was sufficient to cause Yellow House Canyon to run a stream of clear, cold water a dozen feet wide and a foot deep all the way down its course." (W. C. Holden, in Lawrence L. Graves 1962: 18)

The Shermans moved a house they had built in Estacado to the Lubbock County ranch, hauling it on the back of wagons. It was a simple frame house without insulation, and Grandmother Curry, a child at that time, remembered it as very cold in the winter. When Joe had to be gone on roundups and cattle drives, Lina stayed alone with the children. She had to stake out the milk cow and horse during the day, then bring them back in the evening and milk the cow. There were no close neighbors, so Lina had been provided with a gun "and knew how to use it." (Bennett Kerr interview, 2004)

Joe Sherman with sons Forrest (left) and Roger circa 1895. Photo courtesy Martha Marmaduke and Barbara Whitton.

In 1892 Max Coleman was on a horseback trip that took him toward the canyon country north of what is now Lubbock, Texas, and decided to stop at the Sherman ranch for a visit. He found Joe burning the M-Cross brand on a bunch of cattle he had just purchased.

> "A typical frontiersman, [Sherman] gave us a cordial welcome, immediately killing a fat beef, and we spent almost the entire night in discussion, as was the custom at that time.... Through the years, I was closely associated with Joe Sherman and developed a great friendship and admiration for him. Thousands of miles we rode together, several times going up the trail to Hereford and Bovina [small towns in the Texas Panhandle], shipping cattle to Kansas City. On those trips I always skillfully arranged to stand night guard with Joe Sherman. I never tired listening

to his describing his early life. . . . I remember that in fencing his pasture, Mr. Sherman had trapped a beautiful bay mustang pony, which he broke for a saddle horse, riding him many years thereafter . . . . I have often wondered what ranch in Southern Texas lost this horse to some warrior of Quanah Parker. On this horse Mr. Sherman would cover the ground at six miles an hour for the entire day.

"He always carried what was called a California rope. That was a sixty-foot coil of hard manila rope on the right side of his saddle. He could also skillfully throw it, being one of the best men with a rope I ever saw. The usual rope carried in the [1890s] was only thirty-five feet. [Sherman's] long coil of rope was a style of rope which came from California. However, I never saw a longer coil of rope carried than that of Joe Sherman, when I worked on the Miller and Lux Ranch in Lower California, where the Mexican vaqueros prided themselves on their long coils of rope." (Coleman 1952: 138-40)

Coleman describes the Sherman family as "estimable, successful and well-thought-of citizens, being worthy descendants of that hardy, intrepid pioneer, Joe Sherman, who helped settle Lubbock County in the [1890s]." He also says that in February of 1891, he and Joe Sherman were among a small group of people who gathered to celebrate the founding of Lubbock County, on the spot that would later become the town square of Lubbock. The crowd included several of Joe's cowboy chums from Crosby County (George Wolfforth, Will Sanders, Van Sanders, and Rollie Burns), as well as Joe's brother-in-law, George Singer. (Coleman 1952: 83, 140) Joe Sherman, who craved solitude, wouldn't be proud to know that Lubbock has bloomed into a cosmopolitan city of two hundred thousand.

This account by Max Coleman doesn't fill in all the blank spaces in Joe Sherman's life, but it does yield some good information. Obviously, Coleman not only liked Sherman but had a high respect for his skills as a cattleman, horseman, and roper—and Coleman comes across as a man whose opinion should carry some weight. He had spent his youth trapping and breaking wild mustangs and knew what he was talking about. But his observation that Joe Sherman carried a sixty-foot "California" rope baffles me. If Sherman carried a rope of that length, it means that he had come in contact with the vaquero-style of roping, featuring a huge coil of rope that was "dallied" (wrapped) around the saddlehorn, instead of being tied hard-and-fast to the horn, as most Texas cowboys did.

It is hard to express just how unusual this would have been. If you look at old photographs of Texas cowboys who worked the prairie country between Palo Pinto County and the northern Texas Panhandle, you will *never* see a man carrying a rope that even approaches sixty feet in length. As Coleman points out, the longest ropes might have been thirty-five feet. To find ropes of greater length, you would have to go to states where the vaquero-style of roping had taken hold: California, Arizona, or Idaho, or Montana, which drew cattlemen from California as well as Texas and had both roping traditions in place. The Montana cowboys in Charlie Russell's paintings carried big coils of rope and dallied to the horn. (For a more detailed discussion of roping styles and traditions, see my *Catch Rope: Long Arm of the Cowboy*).

Is it possible that Coleman wasn't a reliable witness? I have crosschecked some of his information by consulting other sources and have found very few errors. I take him at his word, and so did Professor Curry Holden of Texas Tech University, who read the Coleman book in manuscript and wrote the introduction. He spoke of Mr. Coleman's "astonishing ability to remember" small details about horses and people he had known sixty years in the past. (Coleman 1952: introduction)

We also have some corroboration from Lina Sherman's first-cousin, Charles Singer, who said that Joe Sherman "could catch wild horses where others couldn't with that sixty foot rope." (Charles Singer interview, 1982)

Coleman recognized that Joe Sherman's roping technique was something unique, but he didn't ask the obvious question: Where in heaven's name did Joe Sherman learn to rope in the vaquero style? Surely not in Texas. There was the year he spent in Nebraska, but Nebraska was no more a vaquero state than Texas. This leads me to speculate that at some point in those years after Sherman ran away from home, he must have spent some time in a state that had a strong vaquero tradition of roping: California, Arizona, Idaho, or Montana. But once again, Joe Sherman has managed to hide his tracks.

My suspicion is that Coleman knew the answer but, for reasons unknown, chose not to reveal it. He seems to have known a great deal about Joe Sherman, including how he died, but he didn't discuss that either. He said only that Joe died in Gaines County June 2, 1917 and that he "well remembered the grief we all felt in Lubbock when we received the sad news." (Coleman 1952: 139)

Chapter Eleven: The Sherman Family

My mother's first-cousin, Roger Joe Sherman, described his grandfather as:

> "…strong, exceedingly masculine, and over six feet in height. His face was spare, sharp-cornered, and intently serious and it matched his disposition. Although he usually walked stiffly and with short steps, he possessed a certain agility and could, when necessary, be quick and cat-like." (Roger Joe Sherman 1985: 16)

Grandmother Curry remembered that in the early years of their marriage, Joe and Lina enjoyed each other's company and seemed very compatible. There was laughter in the house and Joe tried to lighten his wife's load of housework. In the mornings, he would rise early, build a fire, grind the coffee, and start breakfast. When the babies arrived, he was kind and attentive. In the fall of the year, he would ride the train with his cattle to the Kansas City market, and while there, he enjoyed shopping for Lina and the children. For Lina, he bought leather gloves, pretty hats, warm slippers, and bolts of cloth. Grandmother Curry remembered him bringing her an amethyst ring and a little cup and saucer. But as the babies grew into teenagers, discord crept into the home. In her later life, Grandmother Curry admitted that she was stubborn and willful,

Sherman family circa 1908. Front row from left: Mary, Joe, Burt, Lina, Olive. Back row from left: Roy, Mable, Forrest, Roger. Photo courtesy Martha Marmaduke and Barbara Whitton.

and said that Uncle Forrest was too. Joe Sherman had difficulty coping with rebellious children and began withdrawing into a brooding silence. (Bennett Kerr interview, 2004)

As they grew older, his children viewed him as aloof and stern, a man whose anger you didn't want to arouse and with whom you wouldn't want to spend a few years on a desert island—unless, of course, you shared his passion for silence. He seems to have had a temperament that darkened with age and drought, perhaps a genetic curse thrown his way by his father.

My mother said that Joe's early years had done little to prepare him for family life: the murder of his mother and untimely death of his father; being shuffled around from relative to relative, always the step-child no one really wanted; and then his formative years in the Loving camps, tutored by bachelor cowboys who, one speculates, were there at least in part because they lacked the social skills to be somewhere else.

Max Coleman seems to have gotten along well with him, but Max had spent his youth trapping and breaking wild mustangs on the lonesome sweep of the Llano, and had the ability to deal with long periods of silence. We don't know how many wordless hours he had to wait before Joe Sherman was stirred to tell a story about the old days.

As he grew older, Joe Sherman wasn't a loveable man, but on the frontier, that wasn't uncommon or even a bad quality. Once again, John Graves says it well:

> "Sharp around the edges, not tender… They couldn't have been, bringing wagonloads of women and kids and chattels where they brought them. Like the Comanches, they were unlovable to neighbors of other breeds, but like the Comanches too they did not care." (John Graves 1960: 25-6)

The men who survived drought and Indians and horses that were serious about wanting to kill anyone who approached them—those men had qualities of spirit that, today, we would find harsh. Or "insensitive," to use the popular term.

No doubt Joe Sherman was insensitive. So were Charles Goodnight, Sul Ross, Billy Dixon, the Slaughters, the Lovings, and all the other men who left deep tracks on the frontier—not to mention Quanah Parker and his Comanche companions. Men who were sensitive cried sensitive tears while their wives were being raped, and drowned their guilt in saloons while their children went hungry. Maybe Ezra Sherman was a sensitive man and maybe being sensitive in that time was another name for careless . . . or stupid.

The very qualities that made Joe Sherman seem distant to his children allowed him to raise beef cattle in a hostile environment, survive the droughts of 1885-7 and 1893-4, the ferocious blizzard of 1886, and the financial panic of 1893, pay off his ranch, and provide a home for six children who survived into adulthood and became productive citizens. Joe's hard nature served as a shield for Lina, allowing her to bring warmth and love into the home. Joe loved his family and showed it through actions, not words or gestures: he kicked the wolf away from the door, and those who kick wolves don't always have the luxury of being sensitive.

Ahorseback, Joe Sherman was a master of his craft. "He was completely at ease around livestock and sat a horse with the posture, assurance, and grace of a parade marshall." (Roger Joe Sherman 1985: 16) He kept a tidy place and was fastidious about details. He saw to it that every wooden surface on the place wore a fresh coat of paint. In his work, he aimed for perfection and had little patience for incompetence and shoddy methods. For the older boys, he was a hard, demanding master. (Bennett Kerr interview, 2004)

Inside the house, he seemed remote, letting Lina handle the squabbles of the children and the details of running the house. Mother said that he subscribed to the *St. Louis Post-Dispatch*, and read every issue from cover to cover, even though the news would have been weeks old by the time it found its way to Seminole and the ranch. I have wondered why he chose to read a paper from St. Louis, instead of one from Dallas, Fort Worth, Abilene, or San Angelo. Did he want a source of news from outside of Texas, or did the St. Louis paper give a more complete summary of the cattle market at the Kansas City stockyards? We don't know, but by Mother's account, when he was inside the house, Joe Sherman spent a good deal of his time concealed behind a page of newsprint, while Lina mothered and fussed and did her best to make the ranch house into a home. And apparently she did it very well. Uncle Roger Sherman recalled that his mother kept the house:

". . . immaculately clean, and as she did her housework, she sang. In the evenings when the supper dishes were put away, she would gather her children about her for Bible stories. In those quiet interludes, Lina's contagious contentment frequently infected the whole household." (Roger Joe Sherman 1985: 16)

I have a few hazy memories of Lina from visits we Ericksons made to the Sherman ranch in the early fifties: a sturdy ranch woman in a long cotton dress, reaching work-thick fingers into a bucket and scattering grain for her flock of chickens. The thing I remember most about Great-grandmother Sherman was her chicken and noodles. She made the noodles from scratch, rolling them out with a rolling pin. They were thick and chewy, and she added them to the gravy from a chicken whose neck she had wrung herself. I must have been eight or nine years old, and it impressed my little boy's mind that this gentle lady was so adept at executing chickens. It was the sort of thing I couldn't imagine

Mable and Roger as children in Lubbock County. Photo courtesy Martha Marmaduke and Barbara Whitton.

Grandmother Curry doing, she being the epitome of manners and propriety, although I am sure that while raising five daughters during the Depression, she beheaded many a chicken. No doubt she considered it distasteful and unladylike, and she shed no tears when Piggly Wiggly came to town and began offering whole chickens that somebody else had killed and plucked.

One of the stories Mother told me about Grandmother Sherman was especially vivid. One day in the fall (Mother's stories never had specific dates, so let's guess that it happened in 1915), Lina was out picking okra in the garden at the ranch, assisted by the sixth of her seven children, a girl of fifteen named Olive. Olive didn't see the rattlesnake hiding among the okra plants, and the snake struck, biting her on the calf. In those days, the accepted remedy for snakebite (now out of favor) required that someone apply a tourniquet above the bite, slowing the flow of blood to the heart, then carve an X with a knife or razor into each of the two puncture wounds and suck out the poison. Olive had been raised on a ranch that had plenty of rattlers and she should have known what to do: sit down, stay calm, grit your teeth, and look the other way while a rescuer went through the gory process of trying to save your life.

But she flew into a panic and ran, while her mother screamed, "Olive, stop! Don't run, you'll spread the poison!" Olive ran blindly, wildly. Grandmother Sherman's response still strikes me as remarkable, even for a woman who had been raised on the frontier. She ran after the girl, tackled her, threw her to the ground, ripped off the hem of her petticoat and wrapped it around Olive's leg, above the knee. Then using a kitchen paring knife, she carved two X's into Olive's flesh and sucked out the poison with her mouth. Such actions require a special category of grit, but I doubt that Grandmother Sherman considered it anything special. It was just one of those things a mother had to do to protect her children. I'm sure she was aware that the first funeral in Estacado had been said over the body of Mary Ellen Cox, a girl who had died of a rattlesnake bite. (Spikes and Ellis 1954: 254)

Aunt Olive survived, apparently with no serious consequences, although Mother said that every year in the fall, around the day when she had been bitten by the snake, her leg would swell.

Chapter Twelve: Rachel and George Singer

The most famous of our kinsmen was a man named George Singer, who married Lina Sherman's sister Rachel Underhill and was thus Grandmother Curry's uncle. "Famous" is a relative term, of course, and nobody in Los Angeles or New York has ever heard of him, nor have they in Dallas or Houston. But around Lubbock and the South Plains, George Singer is still remembered as a man of considerable importance. His credits include: first merchant in Crosby County (1881), first merchant in Lubbock County (1881), and one of the original founders of the city of Lubbock (1891). Today, a stone marker in Lubbock honors him. It says that he established his trading post in 1877 and local lore tells that he traded with Comanches and buffalo hunters. Max Coleman, who knew the Singers well, claimed that George had come to the region as early as 1870 (Coleman 1952: 59), but the usually reliable Max got his dates wrong. Nobody but the Comanches occupied the Llano in 1870. J. Evetts Haley had Singer located at the crossing of two military trails near Yellow House Canyon in 1879 (Haley 1967: 47), but that date also appears to be incorrect.

A close accounting of events finds George Singer arriving in Estacado with the second migration of Quakers in 1881. (Spikes and Ellis 1952: 34) There, he opened the town's first store but soon moved his operation thirty miles west to the headwaters of Yellow House Canyon, a few miles north of present-day Lubbock. (Seymour Conner, in Lawrence L.

Graves 1962: 55 and 66). By that time, the buffalo had disappeared and whatever Indians happened along were a rag-tag collection of renegades, wanderers, hunters, and beggars from reservations in Oklahoma and New Mexico.

The Southwest Collection at Texas Tech has a taped interview with George Singer's son Charles, made in 1981 when Charles was ninety years old:

> "My folks told me about the Indians coming now and then, renegades from the reservation. Mother had a big wooden chest and when the Indians came, she would put us kids inside. One time there was sixty of them and they camped between the store and the house. They wanted something to eat, so Mother made them some biscuits. Father went to the store and got a big bag of prunes. Mother fed them biscuits and stewed prunes. When they left, about two hours later two of them brought back half a beef and left it for us. " (Charles Singer interview, 1981)

George Singer traded with Indians, all right, but they were not the same Comanches who once ruled the Plains and struck terror in everyone who encountered them. During the 1880s, "Singer's Store was not only the sole house in this vast county, but it was the most important place," (Coleman 1952: 59) a gathering spot for ranchers, cowboys, former buffalo hunters, and travelers on the old Mackenzie Trail. Max Coleman left us a nice description of the store:

> "In my mind's eye I can see old man Singer in his store. . . . An old-time buffalo gun lay on the counter, handy to his hand. Outside, several greyhounds howled for meat, and nearby several wild horses were on the stake. That symbolized old man Singer. . . . I was surprised at the enormous stock carried by Mr. Singer. . . . [He] carried everything. Sacked grain, harness, sacked potatoes, and barrels of flour were piled among boxes

containing Arbuckle coffee, lard, beans, and canned goods. Mixed therein were saddles, boots, bridles, blankets, huge boxes of ammunition, and overalls, and coils of manila rope. Bull Durham tobacco sacks with papers attached were prominent, as that was before the day of the ready-made cigarette. I was surprised at the large amount of candy in the store. Mrs. Singer stated the cowboys were heavy buyers thereof; and, as for the Indians, [George] had to guard them off with a gun." (Coleman 1952: 59, 60)

Rollie Burns, one of the first cattlemen to enter the region, paid a visit to Singer's Store in 1881:

"In and around the store was a motley crowd of cowboys, a few Mexicans, and a half dozen Apache Indians. I mailed my letter, bought a drink of whiskey and some candy, stood around a while, and started back [to the Spur ranch]." (Holden 1932: 73-5)

Because George Singer came to Texas with his wife's family, the Underhills, I had always assumed that he belonged to the Quaker faith. But in his 1981 interview, Charles Singer said:

"My dad was the only one in that [Estacado] bunch who wasn't a Quaker. He was a German Lutheran. He never joined the Quaker church and stayed Lutheran until he died. When I was a boy, I was the only one who would go with him to his church. The service was in German. [The Lutherans] were very different from the Quakers. The preacher smoked cigars. They even danced in their church! Quakers thought you'd go to hell if you even had a deck of cards in your pocket." (Charles Singer interview, 1981)

George and Rachel Singer family, date unknown. Photo courtesy Southwest Collection, Texas Tech University.

So Rachel Underhill, like her sister Lina, married outside the faith, and like her sister, she married a man of action. George Singer appears to have been a tough old bird. Remembering his father, Charles Singer said, "He wasn't a big man but he was brave. He was a westerner, wasn't afraid of anything." (Charles Singer interview, 1981)

In 1886 his courage received a stern test, and there are several versions of the story. Rollie Burns said that "a demented Mexican" burned the store one day while Singer was away. George returned just as the Mexican was fleeing from the building. "He killed the Mexican, but was unable to save the store." (Holden 1932: 195) Max Coleman describes the man as a former comanchero who disputed Singer's right to settle on the headwaters of Yellow House Canyon, an important source of fresh water in those days. Max says that Singer shot the man dead with the large-bore rifle he kept on the counter, "thus settling the matter." (Coleman 1952: 59)

Charles Singer, the merchant's son, gave a detailed account of the incident in his 1981 interview. He said that one evening a party of freighters parked their four wagons near Singer's Store and were having supper when a Mexican man rode up on a mule. He seemed pleasant and friendly, so they invited him to share their meal. After the meal, he saw their guns lying nearby and seized them. He ran the freighters out of their own camp, shot at them, and burned their wagons. Then he broke into the store, started a fire, and began shooting at Singer's house a few hundred feet away.

> "My [baby] sister was lying in a chair and one of those bullets hit a pillow on the chair. Dad grabbed his gun. It was a buffalo gun, .44 Winchester. The man was standing in the door and Dad shot, hitting the door casing, and the man went back in the store. Dad said he walked out to make sure the man didn't come out either door. He wasn't sure if he shot him or wounded him. He never did come out. He burned up in there. There wasn't anything left of him to bury. That store was full of ammunition and kerosene. It made a terrible fire." (Charles Singer interview, 1981)

Charles Singer's sister, Pearl Singer Debler, was emphatic in saying that her father *didn't* kill the comanchero.

> "My father did not shoot the man who burned his store. . . . The man stayed in the store and was burned to death. My father did shoot, but only . . . to keep him from coming out and shooting the family. . . . He was never buried right, as his head, arms, and legs were all burned off." (*Lubbock Avalance-Journal*, September 1, 1959)

Charles Singer's account of the story, which he claimed to have heard several times from his father, does not address the question of motive,

Rachel Underhill as a girl, taken in Ohio before the Underhills moved to Texas. Photo courtesy Crosby County Pioneer Memorial Museum.

but the Mexican man must have been powerfully stirred up about something. Or else he was truly "demented," as Rollie Burns believed. My guess is that George did hit the comanchero, either killing him outright or wounding him badly enough so that he wasn't able to leave the building. A man would have to be more than demented to remain inside a burning store, while boxes of ammunition were exploding all around him.

So there was George Singer, a merchant whose store had been reduced to ashes and rubble. He had the money to rebuild the store, but the nearest source of lumber was at the railhead at Colorado City, and he felt uneasy about leaving Rachel alone with the children, when the dead comanchero's relatives might be lurking around with revenge on their minds. Rachel volunteered to go for the lumber and made the hundred-and-twenty mile trip through wild country by herself, driving six horses, two of which were only half-broken, greasing the wagon wheels twice a day, and sleeping in the covered wagon bed at night. (Coleman 1952: 59)

Charles Singer said that one afternoon, as she was making her way across the prairie, she looked back and noticed that she was being followed by a man on a horse. She didn't recognize him and he followed her all day. By the evening, when she stopped to make camp, she had begun to worry. She picked up a heavy cow bone and carried it into the wagon, just in case.

> "An hour later, he stuck his head into the wagon and she let him have it with that bone. That was the last she saw of him. She *dropped* him. She said she didn't go out to see how long he laid there. The next morning he was gone. I had a wonderful mother, a religious mother. She was a wonderful cook and could make a meal out of anything. Ha. She was good with a bone, too, when she needed to be." (Charles Singer interview, 1981)

Rachel returned to Lubbock County with the load of lumber, and she and George rebuilt the store.

Max Coleman expressed my thoughts when he wrote, "I wish in this day of soft living and modern conveniences some women could have heard Mrs. Singer recount to me that trip she made." (Coleman 1952: 59)

Chapter Thirteen: The End of the Quaker Dream

T here was some good steel in those Quakers. I am sorry that I have never had the pleasure of meeting any of the Singers or Underhills, other than Perlina Sherman. As far as we know, they all left the High Plains sometime around 1892 when their dream of Eden on the Prairie had faded to dust, both poetically and literally. Bad crop years played a major role in the demise of Estacado, as the harsh reality of life on the Llano crushed Paris Cox's vision of orchards and vineyards. He had been correct in saying that the soil was deep and rich, but he had underestimated the power of those endless southwest winds to pull the moisture out of every living thing. Coronado and Marcy and the Comanches could have told him, but Paris Cox's dreams didn't allow him to hear it.

Also, the Quakers failed in their attempts to keep the Gentiles at bay.

> "Soon the cowboys on the nearby ranches learned of the settlement with its beautiful daughters. They came courting and won some of the hearts of the fair Quaker damsels, which was one of the disheartening factors that caused the Quakers to disintegrate." (Spikes and Ellis 1952: 259)

Joe Sherman and George Singer had done their parts in this snatching of Quaker girls, and both of them had gotten themselves embroiled in

Quaker church in Estacado. Photo courtesy Crosby County Pioneer Memorial Museum.

shooting incidents that must have confirmed the Underhills' low opinion of the Gentiles. But that wasn't the end of the scandals. Before the Underhills pulled up stakes and left the Texas frontier, they had to endure one more shameful incident, this one involving their own son Charles.

In 1993 my Aunt Bennett Kerr sent me a photocopy of a newspaper clipping (unnamed and undated, but probably around 1945) that showed Lina Sherman embracing a man named Charles Spence. The headline said, "Brother, Sister Reunited In Southern California After 53 Years." I was amazed. Lina Underhill Sherman had a brother named Charles *Spence*? And they hadn't seen each other in fifty-three years? The story under the headline said:

> "Nearly a lifetime ago, 53 years to be exact, a 20-year old boy left his sister and home in Estacado, Texas, to see the world. Colorful Mexico, buffalo hunts on the great plains and gold mining in the western states were among the highlights of wanderings which culminated in California."

So Charles "Spence" was Lina's brother, Charles Underhill, who had been born in Huron County, Ohio, and had moved to Estacado with his family in 1881. But the story didn't address the most glaring question of all: *why had Charles Underhill changed his name to Spence?* In 2004 Aunt Bennett supplied the answer. Uncle Charlie had gotten caught selling whiskey to Indians in New Mexico. Acting on the advice of his brother, he changed his name and fled the state. (Bennett Kerr interview, 2004)

Charles Singer provides a few more details:

> "Uncle Charlie was running a freight wagon and got to hauling the wrong stuff. The Texas Rangers got after him for hauling whiskey. He got on a horse and pulled out of there, went to Utah and changed his name to Spence. He worked on a ranch and married a Morman girl." (Charles Singer interview, 1981)

Aunt Bennett said that Charles "Spence" was a quiet man and never talked about his past. "His children were shocked when they found out his real name was Underhill and that they had relatives in Texas." (Bennett Kerr interview, 2004)

Was Charles Underhill working with George Singer, his brother-in-law, or inspired by Singer's success as a merchant? The curtain of history comes down at this point, leaving us with a dark stage and many unanswered questions. But one thing seems clear: there was more going on in the minds of those quiet little Quakers than one might suppose.

By 1893 the Quaker colony at Estacado had withered away and "all the colonists, save a few families, had moved away from the South Plains." (Seymour V. Conner, in Lawrence L. Graves 1962: 53) Some moved to Lubbock, some to Oregon, and others went to the Texas gulf coast and established the town of Friendswood near Houston, now best known as a bedroom community for NASA's Johnson Space Center.

My kin, the Underhills and Singers, moved to Kansas near Wichita, and apparently they left with few regrets on either side. When I was growing up, we had no contact with the Kansas relatives, even though

Wichita was only a five-hour drive from Perryton, while the Shermans and Currys lived five and a half hours away in Seminole. The problem, apparently, lay in emotional distance, not just miles, and I would guess that the Underhills had come to regret their leniency in allowing Lina to marry the very Gentile Joe Sherman.

We don't know how they regarded George Singer, their Lutheran son-in-law, but he moved with them to Kansas and remained among the Quakers until his death. But even in Kansas, he was haunted by past deeds in Lubbock County. Charles Singer spoke of this in his 1981 interview:

> "I heard it said that my dad left Texas because he was worried about the Mexican man's family taking revenge. When we were living in Stark, Kansas, one day Perry [Charles Singer's brother] came home and said he had heard that a man was in town looking for Dad. Mother was worried and wouldn't let us boys turn on any lights after dark. I asked why. Dad said, 'Well, certain things happened down in Texas that certain people didn't like, and maybe they're looking for me.' He never said what those things were. The next day we found out it was a postal man who wanted Dad to drive a postal wagon. But it goes to prove that somebody was after him. They had threatened him." (George Singer interview, 1981)

Lina Sherman paid a terrible price for leaving the faith, and I can imagine that on deep winter nights, as the north wind clawed at the eaves of the Sherman ranch house, she must have awakened, remembering the smells of Huron County, Ohio, and thinking of her parents in the rolling Flint Hills of Kansas. Aunt Bennett Kerr remembered visits to the Sherman ranch when she was a child. Grandmother Sherman would bring out letters she had received from her sisters, Rachel and Emma, and read them aloud to Mable and her daughters. (Bennett Kerr interview, 2004) They stayed in touch, but at a distance.

One day in 1973 I was hunched over a microfilm reader in Dallas, rolling through dim issues of the *Seminole Sentinel* for the years 1916 through 1920, when my weary eyes, trained by now to spot the Sherman name on a page of dark print, fell upon this notice:

> "Mrs. Joe Sherman and daughter, Miss Olive, accompanied by Mrs. B. B. Curry and children, left Friday morning for Kansas to visit relatives. They expect to be away for a month." (*Seminole Sentinel*, August 9, 1917)

I sat back in my chair and pondered the meaning of those words. Great-Grandmother Sherman went to Kansas to visit the Singers and Underhills, and took her daughters, Grandmother Curry and Aunt Olive. My mother, who would have been five years old at the time, also went. Joe Sherman, the Gentile son-in-law, had died a violent death in May and in her grief, Lina wanted to spend some time with her family. It must have been a humiliating experience for Grandmother Sherman, facing the we-tried-to-tell-you looks of her parents, and as far as I know, she never went back to Kansas.

And so the noble experiment at Estacado came to an end. "They scattered to the four winds on the earth, but like scattered seeds of fine trees, they made beauty spots wherever they went." (Spikes and Ellis 1952: 259)

Chapter Fourteen: Gaines County

Joe Sherman stayed on the Lubbock County ranch for fifteen years. By the mid-1890s the Texas legislature, which had allowed big ranchers like Colonel C.C. Slaughter and his sons, and smaller operators like Joe Sherman, to graze cattle on vast expanses of state-owned land, had begun passing laws that were friendly to farmers. In 1895 the legislature passed the Four-Section Act "which struck a devastating blow at Slaughter and other big Texas ranchers." That same year, the IOA ranch in Lubbock County began selling land to farmers and by 1898 "farmers were steadily advancing by the hundreds onto the eastern South Plains." (Murrah 1981: 84, 87, 103) Joe Sherman was ready to move on.

The antipathy between farmers and stockmen ran hot and deep on the Texas frontier, and Joe Sherman never had any use for a man who would kill good native grass with a plow. Max Coleman also says that Sherman had been losing cattle to rustlers. (Coleman 1952: 139)

A letter from Joe's Aunt Sarrah Clinesmith, who lived near Sayre, Oklahoma, suggests that Joe was feeling restless as early as 1902, and had been looking at land near Woodward, Oklahoma. It also hints that he might have even considered moving his ranching operations to Mexico. (Clinesmith, letter 1902)

In 1905 he made a prospecting trip down to the sand-and-shinnery prairies of Gaines County, a hundred miles to the south, found fourteen sections of land that suited him, and bought the W.H. Brennand headquarters place, east of present-day Seminole.

Uncle Roy Sherman wrote this account for the Gaines county history book:

> "We moved from Lubbock County to the ranch that fall. We left about the first of October and were some eight or nine days on the road as we moved a herd of five or six hundred cows and calves. There were my father, Joe Sherman, my older sister, Mable, my brothers Forrest, Roger, Burt and myself that helped drive the herd. My mother and two younger sisters, Olive and Mary, drove a surrey or buggy and we had a man that drove the wagon and four mules and cooked. This was the first time for Burt or I to be out with a herd or to stand guard around a herd of cattle at night. We had a two or three-day rainy spell on us. We had a large tent that we put up to sleep under at night. We made it through with no loss of cattle." (Gaines County Historical Survey Committee 1974: 464)

Writing about that cattle drive, an anonymous contributor in the Gaines County history book said:

> "Mable helped with the trail drive of some six hundred head of cattle. As one of the older children, she assumed duties which included riding herd day and night with her brothers in whatever weather prevailed. For those of us in this area who know Mrs. Curry, to see the decorous and immaculate lady—the epitome of gentility—riding night guard on a trail drive is hard to imagine." (Gaines County Historical Committee 1974: 286)

If anything, the land in Gaines County was even starker and more forbidding than the flat expanses in Lubbock County. For good reason, it had been one of the last regions of Texas to attract settlers and town

Mable and Forrest Sherman at the ranch, 1911. Photo courtesy Martha Marmaduke and Barbara Whitton.

boosters. When I grew old enough to notice such things, I asked my mother why Joe Sherman had chosen to make Gaines County the last stop on his long odyssey. She said it was good cow country with strong grasses and a healthy climate; and, she added with a smile, it didn't have many people. Terrain and climate that repelled others attracted this solitary man who wanted to be left alone with his cattle and memories.

Aunt Bennett Kerr remembered the old Sherman ranch headquarters:

> "From the front of the house the land sloped down gently to the southeast. Once an orchard had been planted there. The house itself was L shaped with a porch all the way around. The main part of the house contained a large room functioning as a living room, a dining room, and guest room. To the east of this was Grandmother Sherman's bedroom. Beyond the house, they had

a shotgun-type bunkhouse with three rooms. Forrest and Roger moved out there around the ages of eleven or twelve after Roy and Burt came along. The kitchen was in the northwest part of the house. Outside the kitchen was a long counter that included a washbasin as well as a second hole for a big pail to hold water. Above the basin was a rack to hold linen towels for drying hands, along with a soap dish that held a pumice soap bar. They kept the pail full of fresh water. The men cleaned up here before going into the house for meals.

"The house was lighted by a gas system with visible lines running to various light fixtures. At one time they tried an electrical system driven by a wind turbine. Later the REA provided electricity. The house was heated in the living room by a wood/coal stove when I was a child, and cooking was done on a wood stove in the kitchen. The Shermans had two windmills which were extra tall to catch the wind. The milkhouse was a little one-room structure between the windmills. Water was piped in from the windmills into a concrete trough that held crock jars for fresh milk and eggs. Water flowed through the trough into a drainage pipe that went to the tank. This is where the churning was done. Covered by the shade of trees, the milkhouse remained cool. Painted white, it was always kept clean. It was the refrigeration system for the ranch. Chinaberry trees were nestled close to the barn. Beyond the barns to the northwest was a windbreak of assorted trees that Joe Sherman had planted in the early days. By the late 1920s many of these trees were dying from lack of water. Mother told me that some of the trees were eucalyptus, valued for medicinal use." (Bennett Kerr interview, December 25, 2004)

The new Sherman ranch lay in eastern Gaines County, not far from Cedar Lake, an enormous wet-weather lake, five miles long and three

The Sherman ranch in eastern Gaines County shortly after the family arrived in 1905.

miles wide, that for centuries had provided the Plains Indians with one of the few reliable watering spots on the Llano Estacado. By some accounts, Quanah Parker was born near Cedar Lake and in 1936 the Texas State Historical Society placed a marker on the north shore, claiming it as the famous chief's place of birth. (Gaines County Historical Committee 1974: 3. Some accounts claim that Quanah was born near the Wichita Mountains in Oklahoma; see Neeley 1995: 32; Exley 2001: 5)

Once again, we find a crossing of the trails of the Parker and Sherman families, this time in West Texas, hundreds of miles from their first bloody encounter in Palo Pinto County. In 1917 Joe Sherman died only a few miles from the spot where Quanah was born in 1850.

Chapter Fifteen: Mable

On the Sherman ranch in Gaines County, Joe struggled to find a balance between being a good provider and a good *pater familias*. I see him as an old warrior whose battles were over, an aging frontiersman who was trying to adjust to a sedentary existence and to the unexpected results of peacetime: more barbed wire fences, more settlers, more native sod plowed under, family duties, and church attendance, all coming as he presided over the decline of his physical body and felt the cold breath of age upon his neck.

Up in the Panhandle, Billy Dixon was dealing with the same issues. "Many of us believed and hoped that the wilderness would remain forever. Life there was to our liking. Its freedom, its dangers, its tax upon strength and courage, gave a zest to living . . . unapproached by anything to be found in civilized communities." (Dixon 1914: v)

Fifty miles southwest of Dixon's place, Charles Goodnight sat in a rocking chair on his galleried front porch. Too old to work, he listened to the wind tearing at the trees and growled answers to the stream of reporters who came calling to hear his stories. He had decided that being a famous frontiersman was a nuisance.

And over at Fort Sill, Quanah Parker had moved the bodies of his mother and baby sister from Texas to the Post Oak Cemetery near Cache, Oklahoma, ending half a century of separation.

In his youth, Joe Sherman had never known a stable family, and once he had one of his own, he responded to it in wildly different and contradictory ways. On the one hand, he seemed restless and aloof inside the house, a virtual stranger to his own children, but when those children grew into adults and were ready to fly away, Joe did everything in his power to hold them in the nest.

Mable, my grandmother, was the oldest and the first to face the wrath of the father. By 1910 she was twenty-two and restless to leave the ranch that she had begun to see as a trap and a dead end. After receiving whatever schooling had been available, she had stayed on the ranch to help raise and teach her younger siblings. When a young man dared to pay her a call at the Sherman compound, twenty-five miles east of Seminole, Joe Sherman found ways of sending him down the road.

Sparks flew between father and daughter, nasty scenes that sent Burt and Roy and Olive fleeing to their rooms, and caused Lina to wring her hands and wonder if there would ever be peace in a house that contained a mule-headed father and a daughter who had inherited some of that good Quaker steel from the Underhill side. Joe Sherman wasn't a compromiser but he compromised with Mable, agreeing to send her to Our Lady of Mercy Academy in Stanton, a hundred miles to the south.

Stanton (originally named Marienfeld) had been founded by six German Carmelite friars from St. Boniface Monastery in Scipio, Kansas, whom the Church had sent out west to minister to a tiny and far-flung population of Catholics between Fort Worth and El Paso. In 1882 they constructed a two-story convent building on a hill overlooking the town, added an adobe church in 1885 and another two-story building in 1886, which served as a school and a residence for the sisters.

The Carmelite Fathers disbanded in 1897 and sold the property to the Sisters of Mercy, an order of nuns, who turned it into a boarding school for the sons and daughters of West Texas ranchers. It opened in the fall of 1897 and drew students from Big Spring, Midland, Odessa, San Angelo, Lubbock, and even as far away as Menard. ("The Historic Carmelite Monastery and Our Lady of Mercy Academy." Pamphlet

Mercy Academy in Stanton as Mable might have seen it in 1910. Photo courtesy of Martin County Historical Museum and Martin County Convent Foundation.

printed by The Martin County Convent, Inc., Stanton, Texas. No date).

If ranch people wanted their children to receive some polish and education beyond what they might find in a one-room country school, this was the only place within three hundred miles. Joe Sherman hitched up the buggy and drove Mable over the long, sandy two-rut wagon trace that linked Seminole to the railheads on the Texas and Pacific line. By the time he delivered his headstrong daughter to Mercy Academy, he had worked out a plan for her future. After a year at the academy, she would return to the ranch and become the teacher at Sawyer Flat school, sharing her new knowledge of the world with her siblings and other ranch children in the area. Mable probably smiled and didn't argue, but she had other ideas. Mother said that she wanted to become a teacher, all right, but in California, not West Texas.

If Mable Sherman was an example of the quality of students they produced at Mercy Academy, it must have been an impressive place. The woman I knew as Grandmother Curry had a dignity and bearing that never suggested any taint of rural origins. Erect in posture, direct of gaze, informed, witty, and always immaculately groomed, she spoke flawless English and had a special set of frown wrinkles that were invoked when those in her presence misused the language. Into her eighties, she wrote letters that would be the envy of any college graduate: words written in a precise hand, lines that couldn't have been straighter if they had been laid out with a ruler, and whole pages that contained no misspellings, ink smudges, coffee stains, or cross-outs.

When cowboys entered Mrs. Curry's house in later years, they removed their hats, wiped the cow-lot dust and manure off their boots, and parked their cigars and quids of chewing tobacco on the porch. At her table, they groped their way through a strange litany of manners,

Always a proper lady, Mable Curry stood out in a crowd of cowboys at Buck's brandings on the Jones ranch, circa 1940. Photo courtesy Martha Marmaduke and Barbara Whitton.

taking their cues from Mrs. Curry on how to hold a fork or a china cup of coffee. They kept their elbows off the table, spoke in hushed tones, and curbed their instincts to gulp, smack, and belch. When she entered a room, men rose from their chairs and somehow they knew that their standards of behavior would have to ascend to her level. She didn't preach or lecture about it. She didn't have to say a word. The men knew. Outside, the wind might be shrieking and the sand might be buckshotting against the window glass, but inside was a piece of civilization.

I don't know where Grandmother acquired this aura of dignity. Aunt Olive didn't have it, and it certainly didn't show up in her cowboy brothers, Burt and Roy. Surely some of it, maybe most of it, appeared during that year with the Sisters, who came from a cosmopolitan mix of backgrounds and nations: Ireland, Germany, Poland, England, and Mexico. At the Academy, she studied Bible, grammar, literature, Latin, manners, quilting, sewing, and dancing. Grandmother never talked to me about her year at Mercy Academy, but it must have been a happy time, a period of expansion when she caught glimpses of a world that didn't include sand, shinnery, or wind. And when Joe Sherman came to Stanton in the buggy to take her back to the ranch, I would guess that she had a premonition of what lay in the future. The Academy had not prepared her to live under her father's rule or to teach his children in a one-room schoolhouse.

But a young woman in those days had few choices. Mable stayed at the ranch and she taught and she waited for a chance to escape. The opportunity came one day when a young fellow named Bascom Burl (Buck) Curry paid a call at the Sherman ranch. He was out on a drive through the county, stopping his buggy at ranch houses to drum up support for his run for the office of county clerk.

Curry was a bachelor in his thirties, and a very handsome devil he was. A photograph shows him dressed in a white linen suit, with thick black hair and a pair of dark intelligent eyes. (A Curry relative has suggested that the dark eyes came from a Cherokee grandmother back in Mississippi). There was power in his gaze.

Buck Curry in his white
linen suit, around 1910.
Photo courtesy of Martha
Marmaduke and Barbara
Whitton.

Joe Sherman probably wasn't impressed that Curry worked as a cashier in the First State Bank of Seminole (ranching would have been much better), but they liked each other from the start. When Sherman found out that Curry was a reader, they retired to the front porch and Buck had no chance to talk about county politics. Joe wanted to hear the latest news of the world and then what kinds of books Curry enjoyed reading. I would imagine that Sherman noticed that with only four years of formal schooling, Curry had managed to give himself a broad education in history, geography, and politics, and could hold his own in discussions of current events, animal husbandry, and range management. Sherman was having such a grand time that he paid no mind when Mable came out on the porch with lemonade and cookies, and he didn't notice the way Buck stared at her before she went back inside.

The next time Buck Curry showed up at the ranch, he didn't come to discuss world events with the old man, but to spend time alone with

Mable. Joe Sherman's opinion of him changed instantly. Now he couldn't find a good word to say. Curry didn't belong to one of the local landed families. He was an outsider, a newcomer, who had drifted in from Milam County and had worked as a carpenter. What did he have to offer a woman? Nothing.

Furthermore (and this was a big issue, not only with Joe but also with the rest of the family), Curry had a flamboyant air that grated on the sensibilities of the Shermans. That white linen suit was gaudy enough, but they had even heard whispers in town that Curry went around in the winter wearing a *coyote skin coat*! When Curry sneezed, you could hear him all the way to Lamesa, and he had an annoying habit of honking his nose like a steamboat whistle. And the floor of his office at the bank was covered by a huge, tasteless bearskin rug. (Bennett Kerr interview, 1972)

Buck Curry's stock in the Sherman household dropped like a gutted snowbird—with everyone except the one whose opinion mattered the most. Mable. And what she saw was a man with ambition and enough courage to defy the will of Joe Sherman—and to risk a fight with her brothers, two of whom (Forrest and Roger) were old enough and big enough to cause concern. It will come as no surprise that we know very little about the courtship of Buck and Mable. Love affairs seldom got reported in West Texas in those days, least of all when a Sherman was involved. Maybe their courting was stiff and stylized: Buck saw Mable as his last chance to escape permanent bachelorhood, and Mable saw him as a ticket off her father's infernal ranch.

I like to think there was more to it than that. Both had qualities that made them loveable, so maybe they fell in love.

Mother told me that Buck used to play the guitar at ranch dances, where neighbors came from miles around, danced all night, feasted at dawn, and caught up on the latest news. The Shermans attended those dances, the whole family, and Mable, who was graceful and skilled at dancing, rarely had a chance to sit down. But sitting nearby, with one booted leg thrown over the other knee, sat the glowering Joe Sherman.

If a boy held Mable too close or too tight, he got a tap on the shoulder and a cold blue-eyed stare from Big Joe.

Somehow Buck and Mable continued to meet, and one day in 1911 Mable faced her father and announced and she and Buck were going to marry. The old man went into a rage, sputtering about ungrateful children and deceit and no respect for authority, and stormed out of the house. As always, Lina was left to sweep up the pieces and put things back together.

The wedding was held August 9, 1911 at the Sherman ranch, with Lina and the children present. Joe Sherman wasn't able to attend. As my mother put it, "He had to ride pastures that day." And just in case Mable didn't get the point, he disinherited her.

Mable and Buck at the Sherman ranch with the two windmills in the background. The photo might have been taken on their wedding day in 1911. Photo courtesy Martha Marmaduke and Barbara Whitton.

Chapter Sixteen: Joe Sherman's Death

It is hard to fathom that the American frontier period extended into the twentieth century, but it did. When Buck and Mable moved into their first home in 1911, Albert Einstein and Niels Bohr were working out the calculations that would dethrone Newtonian physics and raise profound questions about the nature of time, space, and reality itself, but the citizens of Gaines County knew nothing of such matters. They still heated their homes with wood or coal, read at night by kerosene lamps, milked cows, and traveled horseback or in buggies. Law and order had come to Gaines County, but as we will see, it retained a ragged frontier edge until the 1930s, when my mother was a grown woman. It may not have been the Wild West of Deadwood and Dodge City, but I suspect that Einstein and Bohr would have found it uncomfortable.

Mable was never fond of babies and didn't want to have a big brood of them, but Anna Beth, my mother, was born in 1912, and before Mable was done with childbearing, she would have five daughters: Anna Beth, Mary, Bennett, Jonye, and Drucilla.

Anna Beth was a beautiful child with her daddy's swarthy features and a pair of luminous dark eyes. Photographs of her at the age of three show eyes that are almost eerie in their depth. According to Mother's account, for two years Joe Sherman shunned Buck and Mable, and refused to speak to them, while Lina maintained contact through secret diplomatic channels. But then one Sunday after church, Joe caught a distant glimpse of Anna Beth in her mother's arms and was so smitten by those big brown eyes that he turned to Lina and said, "Mother, why don't you ask Mable to come visit us some time."

Lina opened a new round of diplomacy that finally healed the wound. Mable returned to the good graces of the family, and maybe Buck did too, although I get the impression that the Shermans never quite accepted Buck as one of their own. Joe Sherman's temperament seemed to grow even more somber after Mable left home. Forrest, the oldest of the four boys and the one Joe relied on to help him with the ranch work, was the next to announce his wedding plans, and again, Joe Sherman opposed the match and could find nothing good to say about the vivacious Mary D Ramsey. (She did not use a period behind the letter D in her name). But Forrest stood his ground and the two were married in 1914 at the Ramsey home in Seminole.

I never knew Uncle Forrest or Aunt Mary D, but I've caught tantalizing glimpses of them in an unpublished manuscript Mary D wrote for her grandchildren. Her loving description of Uncle Forrest gives exactly the kind of personal information that the Shermans rarely revealed:

"Forrest L. Sherman was born December 6, 1890 and died July 28, 1947. His height was six feet-three. He had a perfect physique, weighed around 175, held himself very erect, well poised with dignity. He had great muscles of arm and leg, good square shoulders and large head carried high on a sinewy neck. His nose was straight. He had a long jaw and brow wide and high. His steady eyes were brilliant and very blue, very clear, and they never faded with age. He had an abundance of hair, chestnut brown, and he kept it well brushed back from his forehead. He wore the best clothes money could buy and never had boots that weren't handmade and beautiful. He was very handsome. He had big soft hands with a powerful grip and he enjoyed using it when shaking a friend's hand. He was very quick on his feet and was a dead shot. He had an infallible memory and seldom forgot a name or a face.

"When I married him in 1914, he was considered the best cowboy in the whole country. He worked cattle and ranched all of his life. From childhood almost to his grave he loved and used horses. He never used a small animal, had a light touch on the reins, and sat natural, riding with long stirrups. He may have been thrown—the best of riders were—but there is no record of it. He was proud, almost vain, of his horsemanship. Few men who ever lived and rode had better reason to be. He was a lover of nature and a lover of freedom, and the country as a whole seemed to give him pleasures to the extent that he wanted no human company. He wanted no human talk to interrupt his enjoyment of the solitude. He rode often alone, and the mesquite thickets as well as the tall prairie grass seemed to fascinate him. These delicious moments seemed to form a

Joe Sherman works on the family Hupmobile, with Forrest (left) and Roy. Photo courtesy Martha Marmaduke and Barbara Whitton.

mute religious feeling of gratitude for all of the blessings that had come his way." (Mary D Ramsey Sherman manuscript, no date: 4-6)

Forrest left the Sherman ranch and took a foreman's job on a ranch in northern Gaines County. This left Roger, the next-oldest boy, to deal with an overbearing father who was now tormented by the pain of rheumatoid arthritis and the spirit-killing effects of a prolonged drought. In 1916 Mary Sherman, the baby of the family and everyone's darling, contracted pneumonia and died at the age of fourteen, casting a pall of darkness over the entire household. It was an unspeakable loss, this girl who "laughed like a pixie, smiled like an angel, and cried like a waif." (Roger Joe Sherman 1985: 54)

Into this setting of sorrow and shadow walked a man named Dock Billingsley. If Satan had written the script of Joe Sherman's life, Dock Billingsley would have been the perfect character to ignite a fatal spark. We don't know much about him, only that he was one of many settlers who were pouring into Gaines County, buying cheap land and trying to scratch out a living by farming and running a few cattle. The ranch people called them "nesters," a word loaded with emotional fireworks.

"Nester" had several meanings, all bad: careless, untidy, slovenly, unmannerly, ignorant, coarse, common, and not quite trustworthy. Nesters had missed out on all the hardships of the frontier and now they had come to plow up the land in their futile attempts to make it grow crops God had never intended the country to sustain. They weren't horsemen and they didn't understand livestock. They overgrazed their land, didn't keep up their fences, and allowed their skeleton cows to wander wherever they wished. Cowmen had spent forty years living together on the Llano and had learned to abide by a certain code of behavior, a code that served as law before the law arrived. To the old cattlemen, the code remained the highest law even into the twentieth century, ranking just a few notches below the Ten Commandments and the Golden Rule. Nesters knew nothing about the code.

The death of fourteen-year old Mary Sherman in 1916 cast a pall of darkness over the Sherman home. Photo courtesy Martha Marmaduke and Barbara Whitton.

IN LOVING REMEMBRANCE OF

Mary Nola Sherman,
Born Oct. 17, 1902.
Died Feb. 29, 1916.
Age 13 yrs. 4 mos. 12 days.

GONE BUT NOT FORGOTTEN

We have lost our darling Mary
She has bid us all adieu:
She has gone to live in heaven,
And her form is lost to view.
Oh, that dear one, how, we loved her!
Oh, how hard to give her up!
But an angel came down for her
And removed her from our flock.

Copyright 1898 by H. F. Wendell, Leipsic, O.

In my boyhood, when Mother wanted to shame us for untidy rooms or disgraceful behavior, that was the word she chose: *nester*. In the homes of Sherman descendants, you didn't want to be lined up with the nesters. (It is worth mentioning that I have been a guest author in many schools on the South Plains: Lubbock, Ralls, O'Donnell, Kress, Seminole, Levelland, Whiteface, Earth, Lockney, Plainview, and others. There, I met teachers, parents, and students who were surely descended from people the Shermans called nesters. I found them to be fine people and have wondered what all the fuss was about).

Stories vary on what caused the collision between Joe Sherman and Dock Billingsley: an argument over a waterhole, Billingsley's mistreatment of Sherman livestock, bad fences, straying cattle, or maybe all of them at once, made infinitely worse by drought conditions and Joe's declining health. Writing to her grandchildren, Aunt Mary D Sherman spoke of the incident:

"The Shermans were thought of as the very finest of people. Mr. Sherman was one of the few who acquired his holdings honestly. He took nothing from the other man and wanted nothing from the other man. He was just a man that no one could interfere with. This sort of characteristic existed with a good many of the pioneers and caused trouble and killings when the country began settling with a class of people we called 'nesters.' They were home seekers and entitled to their rights, but it was very hard for a man who had developed his ranch holdings, pastures, and water tanks to see these people take over by state land filing. Mr. Sherman was shot and killed by one of these people. It was just a change of times, hard for me to explain. The man (Billingsley) took possession of one of (Joe Sherman's) best watering places." (Mary D Sherman manuscript, no date: 1)

One day in the spring of 1917, Roger Sherman exchanged heated words with Billingsley in the pasture and most likely both said more than they should have, and more than they actually meant. Roger was a young man trying to protect the interests of his family, while Billingsley tried to cover his fear of the formidable Shermans with false bravado. By the end of May, the feud had become poisonous and Joe Sherman sent word to the sheriff to come out and mediate. But the sheriff had more pressing problems in town and couldn't come, so Sherman heaved his aching body into the saddle, and he and Roger rode off to the northwest pasture to check on things. Since threats had passed between Roger and Billingsley, Joe insisted they go armed, Roger with a pistol and Joe with a Winchester rifle. Being prepared was part of the code. Back in 1860, Ezra Sherman had failed in that regard and his son didn't intend to repeat the mistake.

On the north fence between the Billingsley and Sherman pastures, they saw a horse-drawn wagon, with Billingsley working on the ground nearby. The Shermans dismounted and walked to the top of a little hill, where they could get a better view. Then they started walking down the hill toward Billingsley. Billingsley ran to the bed of the wagon, came up with a rifle, and fired one shot. Joe Sherman slumped forward with a wound in his lower abdomen.

My mother's first-cousin, the late Roger Joe Sherman of Dallas, self-published a book about the life of his father, Roger Sherman, in 1985. Roger Joe, who had worked as a journalist and a public relations director for Southern Methodist University, did a considerable amount of research and had access to the incident's only eye witness—Uncle Roger Sherman, who was also the only one of the Sherman tribe who talked about it, and then only with his son. I think it was unfortunate that Roger Joe chose to fictionalize his father's life, instead of presenting it as a standard memoir, but that may have been the way Uncle Roger wanted it told, hedged and vague. At any rate, Roger Joe's fictionalized account is the best we have, at least from my family's perspective. We don't know what story the Billingsleys have passed along.

According to Roger Joe's version, after Billingsley fired the first shot, Roger pulled his pistol and fired back, missed and fired again several more times, all the shots falling short. When Billingsley's rifle jammed, Roger leaped on his horse, grabbed his father's Winchester, and galloped toward the farmer. Billingsley dropped his rifle and shouted, "Don't shoot! I surrender." But when he reached for a pistol in his waistband, which he intended to throw on the ground, Roger thought he was to going to come up firing. He clubbed the man with the stock of the rifle, knocking him unconscious, and tied him with up with his catchrope. When Roger rode back to his father, he realized for the first time that Joe Sherman was badly wounded. (Roger Joe Sherman 1985: 58 ff)

By this time, Roy Sherman had ridden out to check on his father and brother, and he arrived just in time to be sent back to the house to put out a call for the doctor in Lamesa. He also called the sheriff. (The Shermans must have had a telephone by this time). An hour later, Roy came back with a flatbed wagon. They loaded Joe into the wagon and Roy drove him back to the Sherman ranch house. The sheriff came out to the ranch, collected his prisoner, and returned to Seminole, while Lina and the family began a long vigil beside the bed of Joe Sherman, who had lost a lot of blood and was clinging to life by a thread. It isn't clear how long they had to wait for the doctor, but given the bad roads and poor communications of the time, it might have been a day or more.

By the time the doctor arrived, he could see there wasn't much hope, but he did his best. Sending Lina and Mable out of the room, he operated, using Roger as his assistant. Joe lived only a day or two and died on June 2. The funeral service was held the following day at the home of Mr. and Mrs. B. B. Curry. (*Seminole Sentinel*, June 7, 1917)

A story about the incident appeared in the *Crosbyton Review*:

> "AN OLD SETTLER KILLED. Joe Sherman of Gaines County was shot and killed near Seminole last week in a dispute over a cattle trade. Mr. Sherman had many friends among the old timers of this area, having been among the first cattlemen of Dickens and Crosby Counties. In 1889 he was deputy sheriff under Billy Standifer, who was then sheriff of Crosby, Lubbock, Dickens, and Floyd Counties." (*Crosbyton Review*, June 22, 1917)

After the death of their precious daughter Mary in 1916, the Shermans didn't have much to smile about. From left: Lina, Olive, and Joe. This may have been one of the last photographs of Joe Sherman before he died of a gunshot wound.

Later that summer, a Gaines County grand jury listened to testimony in the case. Roger Sherman served as the main witness for the prosecution and gave his account of the incident, saying that Billingsley had fired without warning or provocation. Billingsley claimed that the Shermans had come to get him and that he had fired in self-defense. The grand jury returned an indictment of first degree murder against Billingsley. The Shermans were pleased with the indictment and felt that the legal system was doing its job. They weren't so pleased, however, when Billingsley's attorneys succeeded in getting the trial moved to Lubbock County in a change of venue. The Shermans feared that with the trial set in Lubbock County, Billingsley's attorneys would seat a jury of farmers whose sympathies would favor Billingsley and not an old-time rancher.

Joe Sherman had helped to establish Lubbock County in 1891 but had moved away 1905, precisely because the country was filling up with nesters. (Roger Joe Sherman 1985: 70-72)

The trial date was set for December 3, 1917.

"Quite a number of Gaines County citizens will leave Sunday for Lubbock, where they will attend the trial of Dock Billingsley, who is charged with the murder of Joe Sherman. . . . Those who will attend from this county are C. E. Rollins, John Dublin, Mr. and Mrs. Ed Heath, W. H. Birdwell, N. R. Morgan, B. B. Curry, and the Sherman family." (*Seminole Sentinel*, November 29, 1917)

"Of the twelve jurors finally seated . . . five were ranchers, four were farmers, one a blacksmith, and two were merchants. All twelve had acknowledged that they believed in capital punishment." (Roger Joe Sherman 1985: 75)

Billingsley's attorney hammered away at Roger's testimony and depicted Joe Sherman as a wealthy rancher who was used to having his own way. He should have allowed the law to settle the matter. The jury might have convicted Billingsley on a less serious charge, but they weren't willing to uphold the prosecution's charge of capital murder. Not guilty. The Shermans drove back to the ranch in stony silence and prepared for a joyless Christmas holiday.

This was the story no one in my family would talk about when I was growing up. It was a searing memory they all wanted to bury and forget.

Chapter Seventeen: The Currys

When I was young, it never occurred to me that my grandparents had anything less than an ideal marriage. Marriage problems, if they ever occurred (and we know they did) were not considered a subject that children or grandchildren needed to hear about. But one night in 1970, when I was twenty-six years old and had a family of my own, Mother and I stayed up late, talking in the living room, and she told me some stories about Buck and Mable that I had never heard before. She said that they were not an ideal match. Like her father, Mable was fastidious, while Buck tended to be sloppy in his habits. Both were strong-willed and neither showed much talent for compromising.

Mable wanted to postpone having children, but Anna Beth came soon and was a breech baby (turned backwards in the womb). Local midwives did all they could and finally sent for a doctor in Midland, more than a hundred miles away. He came in a horse-drawn carriage and said that both mother and child would surely die. Grandmother suffered terribly. Finally exhausted, she fell asleep and her body relaxed enough so that Anna Beth made her entrance into the world. Mable took a long time recovering from her ordeal—a "fallen womb," Mother called it—and wasn't anxious to go through it again. But she became pregnant with my Aunt Mary, and the atmosphere inside the Curry house turned frosty. Buck and Mable argued long and loud, and one night in a fit of anger, Mable told Buck she wished she'd never married him. This hurt

Author's mother, Anna Beth Curry, as a baby with her parents Buck and Mable Curry, circa 1916. Photo courtesy Martha Marmaduke and Barbara Whitton.

him deeply, and twenty years later, when my mother was about to marry, he took Anna Beth aside and said, "Don't ever say that to your husband. It's the kind of thing a man will never forget."

Buck and Mable continued to occupy the same house but drifted farther apart. In those days, divorce was almost unheard of, yet they seemed to be moving toward such a calamity. Buck took an interest in a young woman who worked in the bank, and Mother even suggested, to my astonishment, that Mable had her eye on a nice young man. When Buck heard about that, he told Mable to take the children and move out. He wanted a divorce.

Grandmother didn't know what to do or where to go. She couldn't tolerate the idea of crawling back to her father's house, so she wrote to the Mother Superior at Mercy Academy in Stanton, asking if she could bring her two children and work as a cook at the school. The Mother

Superior wrote back, saying that Mable's place was with her husband and in her home, and that she should find a way of saving the marriage. Mable swallowed her pride and remained in the house. Years later, she told my mother that it was the most humiliating experience she had ever known.

Buck and Mable came to a reconciliation in a way they couldn't have anticipated. Little Mary Curry, who was still a baby, came down with pneumonia and whooping cough, and seemed close to death. Buck and Mable kept a vigil at her bedside for twelve days, and by the time Mary's fever broke, they had decided to make a fresh start. Theirs was never a perfect marriage, but they stayed together until Buck died in 1947. (Anna Beth Erickson interviews, 1976 and 1970; Bennett Kerr interview, 1972)

It makes me uncomfortable to write on this subject. My kinfolks have always held tightly to their deepest feelings and have considered such things nobody's business. I respect that attitude, but the story of Buck and Mable would be less than honest if I portrayed their marriage the way I wished it had been, rather than the way Mother and Aunt Bennett remembered it.

Mother said little about Buck's family back in Milam County, only that Mable didn't care for them. Buck's father was "shiftless" (that was a favorite Sherman adjective) and an alcoholic, and Buck's mother was sickly, shrewish, and whiney. Like many of the people who made their way out to West Texas in those days, Buck left home with no regrets. When he arrived in Gaines County from East Texas, he didn't see sand, shinnery, and desolation. He saw opportunity. He came to town with a bag of carpenter tools and helped build Seminole's first house, two churches, and the Lone Star Hotel.

After Buck and Mable were married, Buck served as county and district clerk for several years, but he had dreams and ambition, and public office didn't satisfy him for long. In 1917, he and several investors organized the Seminole National Bank and Buck served as executive vice president. He was also involved in organizing the nearby towns of Denver City, Seagraves, and Hobbs, New Mexico, and served for a time as president of the First State Bank of Seagraves. (Gaines County Historical Survey Committee 1974: 287)

This profile gives us the story of a young man who left a dead-end situation in East Texas, moved west to a raw new land, and found the respectability he had never known under his father's roof. But Buck didn't quite fit the mold of a small town bourgeois, the kind of script that shows a man working hard in the first half of his adult life, then coasting into old age as chairman of the board of deacons and Citizen of the Year. There was a side of Buck that you would have to describe as eccentric. The Shermans had picked that up right away (the coyote skin coat), and Buck's five daughters became well acquainted with it in their teenage years, as it complicated their efforts to fit in and "be normal" in a community where being normal was important.

An unnamed writer left this description of Buck in the Gaines County history book:

> "A big man, Mr. Curry! He held forth in the old red bank building on the south side of the square where there was a monstrous stuffed rattlesnake in the window. When he laughed his booming and hearty laugh, people all around the square smiled and when he sneezed, it was a terror . . . . They feared Buck was catching a cold." (Gaines County Historical Committee 1974: 287)

Buck seems to have enjoyed being outrageous and tweaking the earnest respectability of some of the citizens of the county—among them his Sherman in-laws. While the Shermans tried to distance themselves from the kind of frontier ethos that had led to Joe Sherman's demise, Buck reveled in the western-ness of West Texas. He hunted. He trapped. He raised horses and traded cattle. He skinned his own animals and tanned his own hides, made his own coat out of coyote skins, built spurs on a coal forge, and kept Mable's house cluttered with the treasures he brought home: old saddles, bits, spurs, Navajo blankets, guns, chaps, and musty books. Buck's affection for junky treasures became a flash point in their marriage, especially the hides and stuffed heads he wanted to hang on Mable's walls.

Another flash point was that she didn't approve of his friends. In town, Buck mingled with the solid folk who made good banking customers, but after business hours, he sought the company of men who, in small towns, were politely referred to as "characters." In her later years, my mother was able to laugh about this, but when she was young and trying to fit in with her peers, it caused her embarrassment and great annoyance. One of Buck's friends was a disreputable fellow named Marvin Prindle who made his living trapping skunks. Even if he had taken occasional baths, he would have been challenged to rid himself of the mark of his profession—the socially deadly smell of skunk musk—but apparently he didn't try very hard, and Mable refused to let him inside her house.

The Curry Sisters circa 1929. Buck Curry always wanted a son but had five beautiful daughters. Front: Jonye and Drucilla. Rear: Anna Beth, Mary, and Bennett. Photo courtesy Martha Marmaduke and Barbara Whitton.

Another of Buck's pals was Bill Birdwell. Bill had come to Gaines County early enough to qualify as old aristocracy and to settle into easy respectability, but he seems to have been determined to avoid it. He cowboyed for a while, served as the county hide inspector, farmed, and traded cattle. Buck liked him because he'd led an adventurous life and told good stories. He seems to have been one of those fellows who always happened to be close to the action. We have already noted that he attended the Billingsley trial in Lubbock, and later on, we will find him at the scene of the most sensational murder in Seminole's history.

Mable didn't care that Bill Birdwell told good stories. She noticed only that he dressed like a tramp, and he was another of Buck's friends who never made it past her front door. When Bill came around, he and Buck had to do their storytelling in Bill's pickup in front of the house, while the Curry daughters peeked through the curtains and hissed with indignation. There is a photograph of Bill Birdwell in the Gaines County history book: a skinny old scarecrow with a buzzard's face, slouched against a lamp pole in downtown Seminole. He wears a wrinkled white shirt, probably spotted with drips of food and chewing tobacco, and a sham of a necktie hangs loose at his throat. On his head sits an ancient husk of a black cowboy hat, pulled down to the level of his eyebrows. The cuffs of his dark pants are stuffed into the tops of worn cowboy boots and his fly is half-open. Yes, Mable Curry wouldn't have liked this guy.

Buck made a successful career as a banker, but like many a Texan, he had a dream of owning a ranch and running his own cattle. In 1931 when the Depression fell like a cement wall on top of rural Texas, Buck's bank closed its doors and Buck had his chance to get involved in the cattle business. (Depositors filed suit against the officers and board of directors, but Buck was not indicted). A New York doctor, E. H. Jones, owned a 64,000 acre ranch in the northwest part of Gaines County and hired Buck to manage it for him. As the boss of this big outfit, Curry employed as many as thirty cowboys (the number fluctuated with the season) and looked after 2500 head of cattle. But he faced more than the usual challenges involved in putting weight on cattle and shipping them to market. Hard times had brought back an old problem that had vexed ranchers from the earliest days on the frontier: cattle rustling.

I would suppose that the Jones ranch had a special attraction to cow thieves, since the owner was rich and lived in distant New York. An imaginative thief who might never steal from his neighbors could convince himself that during hard times, a Prince John from New York City could stand a few Robin Hoods doing night work in his pastures. Buck Curry had been hired to look after Dr. Jones's interest in Gaines County and he wasn't inclined to be careless with the boss's assets. The problem grew serious enough so that Buck carried a .41 single action Colt pistol in his car, and Mother said he even kept it under his pillow at night.

Family stories don't reveal much about Buck's activities during the thirties, but in 1943 Dr. Jones sold his ranching interests to the Higginbothem family. My guess is that the combination of drought, ice

Buck Curry as a handsome bachelor-banker, in First State Bank of Seminole in 1910. Photo from author's collection.

storms, rustlers, and market vicissitudes had convinced him that there were easier ways of losing money than investing in hides and horns. If he had spent a few hours browsing in Buck Curry's library, he might have quit sooner than he did. Wealthy British investors had taken an incredible flogging in the ranching business in 1886 and 1887, when a series of winter blizzards reduced their investments to mile upon mile of frozen carcasses, making the dreary business of investing in railroads and public utilities look pretty good.

Dr. Jones sold out and Buck Curry returned to the banking business, more determined than ever to acquire a ranch of his own. Within a few years, he had put together a respectable outfit of eight thousand acres. Mother said that he had a favorite horse named Dollarbill, and she would imitate the way he called the horse to feed, yelling, "Dollar-BILL! Dollar-BILL!" When he rode Dollarbill, he wore a pair of heavy blunt-rowel spurs he had made himself, beating them out of a Model T spring heated in a coal forge. She also said that he was bitten by a horse with rabies and had to take the only cure known at that time, a series of twenty painful shots injected into the navel.

I have often felt a closeness to Buck Curry, even though he died in 1947 when I was four years old. I seem to have inherited his love of ranching, horses, and books, his brown eyes and maybe some of his eccentricity. I've always lusted for a coyote skin coat. I remember feeding cattle with him and bouncing on his knee as he laughed and called me "Sweet Pea." Mother said he used to take me and my cousin Mike Harter into town and buy us ice cream cones at the drug store. When we had coated our faces and clothes with melted ice cream, he would deliver us back to our indignant mothers and disappear.

I have grown closer to Buck through his books than through any personal experience. In my efforts to reconstruct the history of Mother's people, I have sometimes gotten the feeling that I am following a trail that he laid out decades ago, before I was even born, as though he knew that someone would be drawn to those old books in his library and would find the passages he marked with pencil lines, blank checks from the Seminole State Bank, and napkins engraved with "The Currys." It has happened so often that I have made it a joke with myself. Well, Grampy Buck knew I would be looking for this, and here it is. Thanks.

In 1972 when I was preparing to make my horseback ride down the Canadian River, which I used as the narrative thread for *Through Time and the Valley*, I bought myself a bay horse and named him Dollarbill. Then I wrote Grandmother Curry and asked if she might allow me to borrow the Grampy Buck spurs for the trip. She replied:

> "I am so glad and consider it a compliment that you want to borrow your Grampy Buck's spurs. He would be so pleased, as he spent happy hours making them. I am going to give them to you to keep, as I know you would appreciate them.
>
> "I think Dollarbill will be an excellent name for your horse. May he live long and be a real companion. Do you know, one can grow very near to a good horse. They become a companion, a real one. You can talk to them and they seem to understand. I had such a horse once and my dad did too. I'll be with you in spirit all the way." (Mable Curry letter, January 15, 1972)

I wore the Buck Curry spurs on the river trip and rode my Dollarbill. He only bucked me off once. (Erickson 1995)

Chapter Eighteen: Tom Ross

Buck Curry had his problems with rustlers, but he was fortunate that he never had to deal with Tom Ross, who had died three years before Buck took over the Jones outfit. Growing up, I heard many stories about Tom Ross from my mother, grandmother, and great-uncles, but until I reached the age of twenty-eight, I was never sure that he was a real person, that he actually lived and did the things my kinfolks told me about. Then in 1971 Uncle Roy Sherman sent me a recent issue of *The Cattleman* magazine and suggested that I read an article by Mary Whatley Clarke, called "Bad Man . . . Good Man?" It was about Tom Ross, and it supported the family stories down to the smallest details.

In 1972 I nagged my mother into writing down some of her memories of Tom Ross. She wrote:

> "There never was a time when I was not aware of the name TOM ROSS. He was short and heavily built, his head sitting right on top of his wide shoulders. He had at one time been a professional wrestler. There were whispers that he was hiding out from the law when he moved to Gaines County." (Anna Beth Erickson manuscript, 1972: 2)

In addition to his imposing size, he was an accomplished marksman. "It was said that Ross could hit a quail on the wing with a six shooter."

(Clarke article, 1971: 43) A story from Stanton, Texas, claims that when Ross was being pursued by a Texas Ranger named Captain Rogers, Ross shot the bridle reins out of his hands, disarmed him, and suggested that he leave while he could still sit a horse. (*Martin County: The First Thirty Years* 1970: 15)

At a time when ranchers and cowboys had stopped carrying sidearms, Ross continued wearing a gun. Uncle Burt Sherman said that Ross had gotten himself appointed game warden and was authorized to carry a gun.

> "The authorities knew he would carry a gun anyway, and since nobody wanted to cross him, they made him a game warden. He carried a pistol and sometimes used it on peoples' heads." (Burt Sherman letter, 1969)

Grandmother Curry recalled:

> "To those he liked he was the best of neighbors. He was a nice looking man, some say part Indian, a good dancer, good company, and a crack shot. It is said as soon as sundown came, if he were home, he would draw the window shades for fear some stray bullet might come along." (Mable Curry letter, 1969)

Everyone who knew Ross gave the same report: those who didn't cross him found him kind, generous, witty, and charming. Roy Sherman recalled that Ross "had a wonderful personality and was a man that carried a lot of influence. He was a man who could have been a useful citizen." (Roy Sherman letter, February 1970)

But once aroused to anger, he became a different man entirely. "He was liked and feared by everyone in Gaines County. No one deliberately displeased him. He left you alone if you left him alone, but woe to anyone who angered him!" (Anna Beth Erickson manuscript, 1972: 1)

Tom Ross in profile,
probably taken in prison.
Photo courtesy Panhandle-
Plains Historical Museum.

His real name was Hillary U. Loftis, born in Mississippi in 1872. He left home at the age of fourteen and moved west, where he worked in the cattle trade in Texas and Oklahoma. By the fall of 1891, reaching early manhood, "he had developed into a stocky man standing five feet nine inches tall with dark, bushy hair, an aggressive and pugnacious personality, and flashing black eyes that could pierce like steel."

He took a job on the W. T. Waggoner ranch near Vernon, Texas, and rose to a position of responsibility. But he fell into bad company and began branding unmarked cattle with an outlaw named Red Buck. One thing led to another and 1896 he was indicted by a grand jury in Wilbarger County for robbery with a firearm.

"He changed his name to Tom Ross and wandered about for several years, staying in the cattle trade and dodging the Texas Rangers' efforts to bring him to justice." (Bean and Hawley article, 1996: 16)

The year 1905 found him in Gaines County on the unsettled Llano Estacado, the same year the Shermans established their ranch. Uncle

Roy Sherman said that in the fall of 1905, the Texas Rangers came to Gaines County in search of Ross and camped on the Sherman ranch. They didn't find him.

> "A few years after we came to this country, Ross worked on a ranch that joined us on the west. We lost several head of big calves. My father [Joe Sherman] rounded up the cattle and put them in a pasture east of the ranch house. He and my two older brothers [Roger and Forrest] rode each night for several weeks and would fire their guns every mile or so to scare any thief that might be prowling around. We did not have any more trouble after that." (Roy Sherman letter, 1969)

Ross married Trixie Hardin, a good woman from Lovington, New Mexico, and seemed to have gotten a fresh start. With help from his father-in-law, he bought land west of Seminole on the Texas-New Mexico border, and stocked it with cattle—not necessarily his own. In 1920 young Mary Whatley Clarke took a teaching job at a small rural school near the state line, and one of her pupils was Bessie Ross, Tom's daughter and "the apple of his eye."

> "There I met and became friends with the only 'bad man of the West' that I ever knew, and with his family. Of course, I did not know then that he was living a double life. He was a good neighbor and this was what counted in that lonely country. . . . It was whispered around even then that he was a bad man. . . . It was said that he had killed a man in the past." (Clarke article, 1971: 43)

A few years later, Bess and her mother moved into Seminole so that Bess could attend high school, and there they met and became friends with the Shermans and Currys. Mother recalled:

"Mrs. Ross was a small, heavy set, short lady with graying hair and beautiful eyes. Bess was short and had beautiful black hair and the same brown eyes. Bess was a very sweet girl. She was several grades ahead of me. I remember walking to school one day and she had a box of King's Trio candy. No one I knew that age ever had such a wonderful thing as a box of candy like that. I had never seen or heard of King's Trio but they were chocolates with three kinds of nuts in the centers: pecan, walnuts, Brazil nuts. Bess gave me a piece of her candy on the way to school and I thought she was so sweet to share with me. I believe she was not a spoiled child at all." (Anna Beth Erickson manuscript, 1972: 3)

Mother also spoke of an incident involving Mrs. Ross and Uncle Roy Sherman. By that time, Lina Sherman had rented a house in Seminole so that Roy, Burt, and Olive could attend school:

"Uncle Roy said that when he was walking to school one morning, he passed Mrs. Ross's house and she asked him to help her start the car or fix a flat or something, and he did. Tom Ross never forgot this act of kindness and made a point to single Roy out in a crowd to buy him a drink or to make him feel important in some way. Uncle Roy said his friends always secretly or not so secretly envied him because not everyone was treated so nice by Tom Ross. It was such an exciting thing to be noticed by a notorious outlaw and cattle rustler!" (Anna Beth Erickson, 1972: 3)

Grandmother Curry remembered seeing Ross at church. "One night we were attending church services under a large tent with sides rolled up. Mr. Ross was sitting near the edge and when he became bored, he just somersaulted over the back of his chair and walked out." (Mable Curry letter, October 21, 1969)

While his wife and daughter lived in Seminole, Ross stayed out on his ranch and attended to his business interests. He had bought a ranch that fell on both sides of the state line and this proved very convenient. If he stole Texas cattle, he would keep them on the New Mexico side, and vice versa, making it more difficult for the law to catch up with him. He may have also been involved another business venture that has never been mentioned in the published accounts I've read. Mother and the Shermans were convinced that after the start of Prohibition in 1920, Ross was involved in a large operation that smuggled whiskey out of Mexico. It took some effort to reconstruct this episode and when I began my research, I had only one piece of information: a creepy story Mother told me about the day she saw a human skeleton on display in the Seminole jail.

"I was practicing the piano one Saturday morning. Dad called Mother to send us down to the jail to see a skeleton. We dressed and rushed down to the jail, a little building out east from the courthouse. Mary and I went to the jail and there we saw the worst thing, a rather new [human] skeleton with a little meat still on the bones. At that time I must have gone into shock. For weeks I was so afraid and slept between Mother and Dad, and still couldn't sleep. I think the shadow of Tom Ross pervaded the whole atmosphere. The skeleton was finally identified by some dental work done by a dentist in El Paso. The man was a Mexican bootlegger and was known to be carrying large sums of money. He either was doing this for Ross and double-crossed him some way or Ross knew he was going through the country with lots of money and robbed him. The man was shot, his clothes burned on him and he was buried in a shallow grave. The coyotes dug him up and they and the vultures ate the meat off his bones. All would have been well if some cowboy hadn't been riding by and his horse shied away from the skeleton. It was quite a long time before the skeleton was identified, so Ross probably had a chance to hide out for a while. There was no evidence anyway. There never was." (Anna Beth Erickson manuscript, 1972: 4)

A footnote to this story is that Grandmother Curry was furious with Buck for insisting that his daughters view the hideous skeleton. Buck, who always wanted a son but had five daughters instead, probably thought he was just providing the girls with an educational experience.

To corroborate Mother's story about the bootlegger, I spent several days searching through microfilmed issues of the *Seminole Sentinel*, and sure enough, the evidence was there.

"November 23, 1922. SKELETON OF MAN FOUND FRIDAY. Johnson Graham of New Mexico found the body. Sheriff Cobb found a wound in the left temple and a .38 steel jacket bullet. The dead man wore a blue gray coat, blue overalls, and crossbar summer underwear. The remains were on view to the public at the old jail building." (*Seminole Sentinel*, November 23, 1922)

Three weeks later, the *Sentinel* reported:

"Brothers of the dead man, who formerly lived in Artesia, New Mexico, in a statement to the Gaines County sheriff gave the authorities an inside view of a whiskey running ring which is alleged to have been operating between El Paso and the Texas oil fields for the past two years. . . . Further information is said to throw suspicion upon alleged members higher up in the ring. The murder is believed to have been the result of a frame-up, according to authorities, when it was revealed that the murdered man carried with him on the fatal trip 1500 dollars in money and 432 quarts of whiskey en route to Snyder, Texas, where he was to exchange the money and whiskey for a herd of cattle. Car, money, and whiskey disappeared before the murder was discovered. The car was located at Roscoe three days ago by Nolan Co. officers, but the whereabouts of the currency and liquor have not been revealed. The car was specially built, fitted with two sets of license plates for use in Texas and New Mexico, 19 gallon gas tank and a specially built body." (*Seminole Sentinel* December 14, 1922)

The following spring, the *Sentinel* reported that a man named E.C. Lamb had been indicted by a Gaines County grand jury for the murder of the bootlegger, Jim Urban. "Urban was thought to have been bootlegging for Lamb, whose sister is the wife of Anton Classen, the wealthy president of the Oklahoma City Street Railway Company." (*Seminole Sentinel*, April 26, 1923)

Uncle Roy had a clear recollection of these events.

"As for E. C. Lamb, or 'Red' Lamb as he was called, he was indicted for the murder more on being the last man seen with [Urban]. . . . [Lamb] was a member of the whiskey ring and I am sure closely associated with Tom Ross. Ross was generally credited with the killing. Red Lamb died of stomach cancer before he could stand trial." (Roy Sherman letter, February 3, 1970)

As far as I can determine, Ross's name never appeared in any of the newspaper accounts of the murder, and he was never charged. Before the authorities had time to finish the investigation of Jim Urban's murder, Tom Ross had gotten himself involved in another crime, this one truly spectacular.

In the fall of 1922, Tom Ross and his associate, Milt Good, were charged with cattle theft in Lea County, New Mexico, and Gaines County, Texas. The case against the two had been worked by two determined inspectors for the Texas and Southwest Cattle Raisers Association (TSCRA), W. David Allison and Horace L. "Hod" Roberson. You might recall that Joe Sherman's mentor, Jim Loving, had helped organize the

Cattle Raisers Association, whose primary goal was to stamp out cattle rustling.

> "Allison was reputed to be one of the very best peace officers the Southwest had ever produced. . . . Sixty-three years old at the time, he was noted for being absolutely fearless and had participated in numerous gunfights. Roberson's credentials as a lawman were also impressive and he was considered a role model for younger officers in the association." (Bean and Hawley article 1996: 16)

The officers were determined to prove that Ross and Good had been involved in the theft of 485 head of cattle from the Littlefield Cattle Company, a theft on such a grand scale that it was shocking even in those rough times. Roberson and Allison got their indictment from the Gaines County grand jury, although Mother said that people were so afraid of Ross that nobody wanted to sit on the jury. The trial date was set for the following April.

On Sunday evening, April 1, 1923 (oddly, both Easter Sunday and April Fools Day), Roberson and Allison were sitting in the lobby of the Gaines Hotel, having cigars and conversation with a group that included the presiding judge, attorneys for Ross and Good, the district attorney, and Buck Curry's old pal, Bill Birdwell. On his way home from church, Gaines County sheriff F. L. Britton dropped by, unarmed. Mrs. Roberson had come to Seminole with her husband and was upstairs in her room.

Mother described the setting:

> "It was a two story structure with the lobby, dining room, and kitchen downstairs. The lobby seemed quite friendly to travelers, and Mrs. Averitt and her old maid daughter, Miss Beulah, ran both the hotel and dining room. . . . I can imagine how nice and cozy it was on this night, after the roomers had been stuffed with some of Mrs. Averitt's good chicken fried steak, gravy, biscuits,

scalloped tomatoes, cabbage slaw, red beans, and peach cobbler and coffee. They were settled down with the cigars all lighted and ready for some good conversation until bedtime." (Anna Beth Erickson manuscript, 1972: 1)

Suddenly, into this peaceful setting marched Milt Good, carrying a shotgun, and Tom Ross holding a pair of .45 pistols. "Pandemonium broke loose. Numerous shotgun blasts and pistol shots shattered the night air. Neither lawman had a chance to see what was coming" and both lay dead on the floor. The witnesses fled, and as Good and Ross ran from the smoke-filled room, Mrs. Roberson came down the stairs to see what had happened. Seeing at a glance that her husband was dead, she quickly found a small automatic pistol on Roberson's body, "deftly flicked the safety off as she ran to the front door, and fired two shots through the screen door at the fleeing assassins. Marksmanship skills her husband had taught her served her well; she hit both Ross and Good," though both were superficial wounds. (Bean and Hawley article 1996: 17)

I remember Mother saying that the Curry family had just sat down for supper, when Buck heard gunfire coming from vicinity of the town square. He jumped up from the table and cranked the telephone. "Central? What were those shots?" Then he drove down to the square and was one of the first to arrive on the scene. By then, Good and Ross had escaped into the night. With Ross on the loose, "The whole town was in a deep cold fear which I believe was the mood that Tom Ross always put that whole part of the country in. People were deathly afraid of him." (Anna Beth Erickson manuscript, 1972: 2)

Bean and Hawley say that Ross and Good "laughed and joked about the killings, which both considered to be self-defense. Feeling confident they were justified in their actions, Ross and Good returned to Seminole the next day and turned themselves in." (Bean and Hawley article 1996: 17) Ross was convinced that no grand jury in Seminole would indict him, even for such a cold-blooded murder.

On that score, he was mistaken. Both men were indicted and their trials moved to a court Lubbock. "For the first time Good and Ross seemed to realize their serious predicament. Their bravado fell away and their sunburned faces were serious and vengeful. They had not expected to remain behind bars." Dayton Moses, attorney for the TSCRA, assisted in the prosecution and "was under constant guard night and day." Friends of Ross and Good spent thousands of dollars to hire the best defense attorneys in Texas, but both men were convicted. Ross received a sentence of thirty-five years, Good twenty-six. (Clarke article 1971: 62)

They served time at the Huntsville, Texas, penitentiary, but in 1926 the pair made a sensational escape. "Ross and Good fled northward, and after several dangerous encounters and narrow escapes from the law, split company after a mild difference of opinion." (Bean and Hawley article 1996: 17)

Mother said:

> "There were many interesting tales about Tom Ross after that. I remember hearing about how he would come to visit his wife on the ranch. It was said that he would dress as a woman and would come to town to do business, and almost everyone knew who he was but no one would tell. One time he was said to have gone to a place of business and someone recognized him by his small hands." (Anna Beth Erickson manuscript, 1972: 2)

Ross made his way up to Montana and took a job on a ranch. Here, we have two different versions of Tom Ross's last days. Bean and Hawley say that Ross got into an argument with the ranch foreman and killed him. Then Ross burned his personal papers, wrote a short note, spread a tarp across his bed, and shot himself. (Bean and Hawley article 1996: 17)

Uncle Roy Sherman didn't remember it that way.

"To the best of my memory he escaped from the pen in 1926. It is said he came back to this country to see his wife and to pick up his guns that were returned to his wife after the trial. I understand he left shortly for Montana. He worked on a ranch there, where he killed a cattle inspector and was killed, either in January of 1929 or 1930. He was going under the name of Charlie Cannon when he was killed. . . . His body was brought back to this country and was buried at Lovington, New Mexico." (Roy Sherman letters, October 22, 1969 and September 27, 1969)

Grandmother Curry never believed that Ross killed himself. "Many people say he committed suicide but those who knew him will say this is not true, as he was not afraid of the devil and all his angels." (Mable Curry letter, October 21, 1969)

That was the Tom Ross my family knew, and the one I heard so much about when I was growing up. But that's not quite the end of the story.

Chapter Nineteen: Milt Good

Decades after Tom Ross died, people in West Texas and Eastern New Mexico still had strong feelings about him. They liked him, they hated him; he was kind and he was cruel, a good man and a thief, a friend but an enemy, a devoted family man but also a cold-blooded killer. His personality expressed such a fascinating mixture of power and charm that those who shared his company, even at a distance, never forgot the experience. That was not the case with Milt Good. My mother said little about him. Neither did Uncles Roy and Burt, and neither did Grandmother Curry. They talked only of Tom Ross, mentioning Good only in passing, even though Good ranched around Brownfield, only thirty miles from Seminole, and was surely acquainted with the Shermans and Currys.

History has little to say about Milt Good, even though he was charged with being an active, equal partner in the most gruesome murder in Seminole's history. Juries in Lubbock and Abilene found both men guilty of murder and gave them the same sentence—although, in an odd twist, the Lubbock jury deleted nine years from Good's sentence, one year each for the wife and eight children he would be leaving behind. We would have to conclude that Milt Good was a moon that reflected the light of Tom Ross' sun, and like the moon, he spent much of his time in half-light and darkness. So who was he?

In August of 2004 I was working in the archives of the Panhandle

Plains Historical Museum (PPHM) in Canyon, looking for photographs to use as illustrations in this book. I had never seen a photograph of Tom Ross, and on the slim chance that one might exist, I checked the card catalog under "Ross." Sure enough, they had one. When the reference librarian brought me the folder, I opened it up and studied the picture of this man about whom I had heard so many stories. It appeared to be a prison mug shot, showing only the right side of his face: a man with a bull neck, rough skin, thinning black hair, and menacing black eyes. No wonder my mother had nightmares about him. This was a scary man. Curious to know the source of the photograph, I returned to the card file and looked it up again. The notation at the bottom of the card said, "Good, Milt. *Twelve Years In a Texas Prison.*" This was the book J. Evetts Haley had told me about thirty-one years ago, and the museum had a copy of it!

In 1935, after he was released from prison, Milt Good hired a man named W. E. Lockhart to write his story and Good published it himself "to make enough money . . . to buy me a little home and settle down with what is left of my family to the life of a good American citizen." (Good 1935: 5) I don't know how many copies he sold, but it probably fell short of the number that would have paid for a nice little home. The book is rare enough today so that the PPHM keeps it under lock and key, and readers are issued a pair of white cotton gloves before they touch it. I had never seen the book or even known anyone one who had seen it, with the single exception of J. Evetts Haley. At last, I would have a chance to hear Milt Good's side of the story. It is a strange little book, a disjointed scrapbook of reflections on a variety of subjects.

Good begins by giving us a glimpse of his past. As a young man, he cowboyed in West Texas, ranched in New Mexico, and went broke after blizzards and droughts wiped him out. In 1919 he turned to professional roping, or "roping for prizes," as he called it. In 1920 he won the world's championship steer roping at Shreveport, Louisiana. He attributed his success as a roper to the fact that "I never drank any liquor of any kind, never dissipated, and was always in good physical condition." (11) He also trained polo ponies for G. H. Coyle of Midland. (17)

He lists the best calf- and steer-roping horses he ever saw, and describes one of his prison jobs, disposing of the corpses of electrocuted convicts. "I witnessed many electrocutions. They were all horrible." (28) Anyone who has ever wished to rope a buffalo will be interested in this vignette from his days at the Huntsville prison:

"The manager of the Wynne farm had secured two buffaloes and placed them in a corral on the prison grounds. One day they broke through the fence, and Camillo Ramirez and I had the pleasure of roping them and returning them to their places in the corral. Buffaloes are faster and harder to rope than cattle,

left: Milt Good in 1931, dressed for the first prison rodeo that he organized and managed. Photo courtesy Panhandle-Plains Historical Museum.
above: Tom Ross, the man who caused my mother to have nightmares. Photo courtesy Nita Steward Haley Library, Midland.

but if you have a good pony you can outrun and rope them. They will run over anything while you are chasing them, and a good fence will not slow them up in the least. Camillo and I finally roped both buffaloes and returned them to their corral. I think the manager would like to give these beasts away to some individual or institution." (60)

He reproduces letters from people who vouched for his good character, and gives the names of citizens who signed petitions for his pardon, including members of the jury of his Lubbock trial. (87-8) He offers two long lists of friends, including legendary ropers Clay McGonagil, Bob Crosby, and Ike Rude, (14-5) as well as Dolph Briscoe (Uvalde rancher and father of the Texas governor) and Texas Ranger Captain Frank Hamer, a man who was not famous for his love of criminals. (87)

He gives his wife a chapter in which she talks about the hardships she experienced while Milt was in the slammer. He even includes a homily on prison reform. A photograph of Good shows him dressed for a prison rodeo, a slim cowboy with a broad smile and an open, honest face. This is a fellow you might meet at a church picnic. If you ran into him on Main Street, you would buy him a cup of coffee and pass a pleasant hour talking about horses and grass conditions and the cattle market. The contrast between the photographs of Good and Ross is bewildering, and the reader is left with the great unanswered question of this whole affair: If Milt Good was such a nice guy, if he had such a legion of friends, if he had been blessed with a devoted wife and eight children—*what was he doing in the company of Tom Ross on the evening of April 1, 1923, and how did he get himself involved in a gruesome double murder?*

On that subject, the only subject that would have prompted someone to buy and read his book, Milt Good maintains a maddening silence. He claims that several days before the killings of Roberson and Allison, he rode the train to Seagraves to look at a set of steers Ross had for sale. Ross insisted that he stay over and spend a couple of days at the ranch.

"People who know Mr. Ross know that he was a man you could not get away from easily. I rode out to his ranch and spent Saturday and Sunday there; and Sunday evening he took me to Seminole where the trouble occurred. Entering the hotel lobby we found it filled with people; Sheriff Britten, Judge McGuire and his father-in-law, Judge Morgan, the county attorney; Mr. Birdwell; G. E. Lockhart, a lawyer and others. This shooting occurred about 8:00 on Sunday night." (17)

Good's description of the shooting is remarkable for what it *doesn't* say. There is no roar of gunfire, no smoke lingering in the air, no groans of pain, no blood dripping down the walls. We do not hear the screams of Mrs. Roberson as she comes down the stairs and sees her husband dead on the floor. Good covers the entire episode with a single sentence ("The shooting occurred about 8:00 on Sunday night."), giving us only the correct time and day of the week. If you were to diagram his sentence, it would say that the subject of the action (shooting) simply "occurred." Nobody planned it, nobody pulled the triggers, nobody suffered or died. Beyond this, he offers little in the way of specifics.

"More unfounded rumors and untrue reports have been circulated about the killing of H. L Roberson and W. L. Allison . . . than any other case that ever came to trial in the courts of Texas. It is not my purpose to correct them, in fact, it is my opinion that the less that is said about this affair the better. Both inspectors had records as killers and were regarded as dangerous men. (16) Tom Ross and I always felt that we were both prosecuted and persecuted by the Texas and Southwest Cattle Raisers Association, which had employed Dayton Moses as special prosecutor in our cases." (40)

"In the trials that followed the killing, Ross and I pleaded self-defense; and I am still convinced that the plea was justified.

We could have run away from this trouble, but we had both been raised in the West and had not been taught to run from anything or anybody." (16)

He closes the book with:

"The State of Texas and the TSCRA had demanded a heavy penalty of me, and I paid it without whining. I was separated from my family for nearly twelve years. When I entered prison I was a comparatively young man; when I was pardoned I was a grandfather. The punishment that hurt me most was the thought of my family that needed help and I was unable to go to their assistance." (77)

And that's it. He doesn't deny his part in "the trouble," as he repeatedly calls it; he just doesn't talk about it. Maybe, even after thinking about it for twelve long years, he still didn't know what to say. But he does talk about the murder trials in Lubbock and Abilene, and gives a detailed account of his and Ross' escape from prison, so let us allow Milt Good to tell his story.

After "the trouble," Good and Ross stopped at a ranch house outside of Seminole.

"We then drove out to Sune Birdwell's ranch and phoned to the sheriff. He refused to come out, but stated that he would wait at his office until we returned. We returned to Seminole and gave our guns to the sheriff about 10:00. I think that we made a mistake by surrendering that night, because as soon as our guns were out of our possession, things began to happen." (17)

To their surprise, they were denied bail and kept behind bars. They were tried separately, first in Lubbock for the killing of Allison, then in Abilene for the death of Roberson. "At Lubbock we could not understand why so many safety precautions were taken. The jail was guarded day and night by deputies armed with shotguns and every person was carefully searched before entering the court room." (19) When they were driven from Lubbock to Abilene for the second trial, "Our departure from the Lubbock jail was kept a secret, but we could tell by the actions of the sheriff and his deputies that we were to be transferred. We were taken on the train under heavy guard at night from Lubbock." (20) In Abilene, as in Lubbock, the juries found them guilty.

> "We were given every assurance that our sentences would run concurrently, but when we learned that each sentence must be served separately it dawned upon us that we were virtually under life sentence. . . . This should be remembered when passing judgment upon our actions later in efforts at escape." (21)

After the Abilene trials, the two were transported to Dallas to await the actions of the Court of Criminal Appeals.

> "We were placed in charge of J. E. Russell for this trip. He made every possible arrangement to prevent an escape. Three automobiles, each containing three heavily armed deputies, carried us to Dallas. There was a lead car, the center car in which we were double handcuffed and then chained to each other, and the rear car. These cars did not take the usual highway to Dallas." (21)

Good maintains that it was Ross who came up with the idea of breaking out of the Huntsville prison. "The main cause for this escape was Tom Ross' dissatisfaction. We had spent so much money [on legal defense] and felt sadly mistreated. . . . Tom was fifty-five years of age and under sentence of fifty-five years. . . . It seemed hopeless." They escaped with two other men, Red Whalen and George Arlington.

"Tom was working then in the mechanical department and was well liked by his foreman. We had formed the acquaintance of Arlington and Whalen in the Dallas Jail. It was left to me to check sick men into the hospital. This night I checked all three [Ross, Whalen, and Arlington] into the hospital." (29)

Good was able to disarm the guard on duty at the time. Their plan called for each man to do certain tasks, including cutting the telephone wires, and they walked out of the hospital. It appears that they had taken the guard hostage, but Good leaves that vague. "We descended the stairs on the outside and were in a waiting automobile, which had been placed there at our request, within five minutes from the time I had 'mugged' the guard."

In other words, someone on the outside helped them escape. Again, Good withholds the details. "All I have to say now is that there was a man and a woman in that car. It must have been at least thirty minutes before any alarm was turned in. . . . We were some twenty miles away by then." (30)

Leaving the prison, they drove north to Dallas and Albany, and spent the night in the town of Peacock. The next morning, they ate a big breakfast and bought some clothes (no mention of how they paid for these items, or if they paid for them at all), and drove through Spur and Crosbyton to Littlefield, where they read the first newspaper account of their escape. The headline read, "Fleeing Quartet will soon be arrested near Rio Grande."

They made their way to California and Portland, Oregon, where they split up. Ross and Good went to Seattle and to the town of Blaine in British Columbia, where they worked in a sawmill. They began to suspect that they were being watched by law enforcement officers and left town. (30-4) Outside of town, they were stopped by a police car containing three officers. One of them approached Ross, who was driving. "Tom placed a .45 against his ear and told him not to move or speak. I opened the door, stepped out and took the officer's gun." Ross then demanded that the other officers surrender their weapons, and they did. "We marched them down the road about fifty yards and had an understanding with them. . . . They said that if we would not mention the affair that they would not. I think they kept their agreement." (34)

By then, Ross and Good wanted to go home and see their families, so they drove to New Mexico and stayed three days at Ross' ranch, with his wife and daughter. They then drove to Pushmataha County, Oklahoma, where they decided it would be best to split up, as they knew they were being hunted.

"[Tom] said that I was the best friend he had ever had. When he left, I gave him a 30-30 Winchester. As he told me goodbye, he said that the man who took that Winchester from him would take it after he was dead and gone. I never saw Tom again." (35)

Good spent a few days in Oklahoma, hunting and fishing with his brother, and while there he was captured and taken back to the Huntsville prison. (36)

"Tom must have been more clever than I am. He evaded capture successfully and returned to Montana where he assumed the name of Charles Gannon, and entered the ranching business for which he was best fitted. After about three years' labor here trouble came his way again. Perhaps the most authentic story of Ross' death is that told by Edd Regan, a friend who brought the body back to Texas for burial." (43)

According to Edd Regan, Ross got into an argument with the ranch foreman, R. C. Hayward, and Ross shot him.

"The weather was thirty degrees below zero and Ross asked the [other cowboys] to lay Hayward where he could receive medical aid, but Hayward died a few minutes later. Ross then told the boys he was going to take his own life, asked them to feed the horses, went to his room and fired the shot that took his own life." (44)

At this point, Good gives an amazing account of Tom Ross' funeral service in Lovington, New Mexico:

"At the same time that Ross . . . was buried, services were also conducted for his old friend, Walter McGonagil. Three thousand persons, friends and relatives of the two men, assembled from all over Texas and New Mexico for the double funeral. The little church could not hold a fourth of the crowd. Ross and McGonagil who were the best of friends, and had known one another for many years, had last met some eight years ago at the funeral of McGonagil's brother, [famous champion roper] Clay. They had stood over Clay McGonagil's body, put their arms about one another and wept. (44)

"These friends [Ross and Walter McGonagil] were separated by the laws of Texas and only Providence brought them back together, but both were in their caskets. Ross was fifty-nine years old and McGonagil was about fifty-five. After the double funeral, two hearses drove side by side to the small cemetery and the bodies were lowered into their graves at the same time. This caused the greatest assembly of old-time Texas-New Mexico cattlemen that New Mexico had ever known. Cowboys acted as pallbearers for each casket. Gray-haired cattlemen and cattle women stood silently with bowed heads and many bitter tears were shed." (45)

We don't know how many of those tears were shed over Walter McGonagil and how many for Ross. It is hard to believe that the ranch people who had lived in fear of Ross and had long suspected him of being a cattle thief would have felt much grief. On the other hand, we have numerous testimonies of people who admired Ross, both as a cattleman and as a person. Such was the power of his personality that he might have maintained a core of loyal friends right to the end. There is nothing in Milt Good's book to suggest that his admiration for Ross ever dimmed.

In 1927 Good made another attempt to escape from prison but dislocated his knee and was recaptured. (48) He never tried to escape again. In 1931 he made trustee, then worked as a chauffeur for the general manager of the prison system. He also organized the first Huntsville prison rodeo and served as its manager. (59) Outside the walls, Good's wife made seventeen trips to Austin and spoke to three governors in her attempts to obtain a pardon for her husband, and it was finally granted in 1935 by Governor Miriam Ferguson. Mrs. Good says, "The longer the Governor refused to grant my request, the louder I cried. I guess the Governor had to grant the pardon to get rid of me." (78) In this otherwise sordid tale, Mrs. Good stands out in bold relief as a woman of admirable character: honest, brave, resourceful, and loyal, a woman who cared for her children and stuck by her man through hell and high water.

> "When the trouble came into our home, we had eight children, the oldest twelve years of age and the youngest a baby only a few months old. I determined not to break up the home, but to work as hard as I could to keep all the children together. For a while I kept boarders and conducted a rooming house. Lawyers' fees and trial expenses had taken practically all our property. ... My experience in seeking this pardon for my husband taught me to distrust two classes of people—lawyers and newspaper reporters." (72)

I was fascinated that Mrs. Good grew up in Stanton and that when Milt began courting her, "She, the daughter of a frontier merchant, was in a convent." (76) That "convent" was Our Lady of Mercy Academy, the same school Grandmother Curry attended in 1910. They might have been there at the same time and might have known each other, although Grandmother never mentioned it.

Milt Good has left us some interesting tales, but also many unanswered questions. What astounds me most is that one can read the entire book without getting the feeling that Good ever comprehended that the man he admired and whose company he apparently craved—Tom Ross—was capable of monstrous evil.

> "Tom Ross and I were not partners in the ranching business. We were only friends and neighbors. He had come to Gaines County from Lamar County in 1901 and entered the ranching business. . . . He had been involved in some trouble in Lamar County, but had come out of it and (in 1923) was living as a law abiding citizen." (17)

A law abiding citizen? Ross had a reputation for cattle theft that went back at least to 1905 when Joe Sherman and his sons were patrolling their pastures at night. He had a life-long history of violence and intimidation. In 1922 he had been charged with cattle rustling in Texas and New Mexico, and members of my family were convinced that he had killed Jim Urban and left him on the prairie for coyote bait. He *was not* a law-abiding citizen. Milt Good appears to have been extremely naive and gullible, never addressing the fact—undeniable, it seems to me—that Tom Ross ruined his life. He remained loyal to a man who didn't deserve his loyalty, a man Good might have been describing when he wrote of roping those buffalo in prison: "They will run over anything while you are chasing them, and a good fence will not slow them up in the least." (60) One suspects that if he had stayed away from Ross, he would have walked on the right side of the law and fulfilled the promise of his last name: Good.

In a book called *Without Conscience: The Disturbing World of the*

Psychopaths Among Us, Robert D. Hare, Ph.D. writes of his experiences working with prison inmates, many of whom he diagnosed as psychopathic personalities.

Psychopaths are often charming and witty, but shallow. They are selfish, experts at manipulation, and extremely gifted liars. But the most revealing trait of psychopaths, the one that sets them apart from the rest of the human community, is that they have no conscience. To them, robbing, swindling, or killing another human being is nothing more serious than swatting a fly or stepping on a bug.

> "Psychopaths are social predators who charm, manipulate, and ruthlessly plow their way through life, leaving a broad trail of broken hearts, shattered expectations, and empty wallets. Completely lacking in conscience and in feelings for others, they selfishly take what they want and do as they please, violating social norms and expectations without the slightest sense of guilt or regret." (Hare 1993: xi and xii)

Psychopaths are not mentally ill. They know the difference between right and wrong, and they choose to do wrong—because it makes them feel good, because they want to, because they can. They kill people for the same reason they would smoke a cigarette or drink a can of beer, and to them, there is no moral distinction between the two. Normal people cannot comprehend such chilling logic. That is why we find psychopaths so mysterious and terrifying.

Dr. Hare's profile of the psychopathic personality bears a striking resemblance to the descriptions of Tom Ross: charming, witty, intelligent, forceful, violent, remorseless, selfish, and manipulative. Several accounts of Ross mention his powerful eyes and penetrating gaze, a quality that has been observed in Charles Manson and many serial killers. And everyone who knew Ross, including my mother, grandmother, and Uncle Roy Sherman, remarked that he seemed to be two different men occupying the same body, one good and one evil. That is how average people describe a man who has no conscience. Even Milt Good, who wasn't much prone to analytical thinking, noticed this:

> "Tom Ross seemed to possess a dual personality. To his friends he was a kind, lovable man. His door was always open to his friends but closed to his enemies. He was a big-hearted man who would go the limit for his friends and give his last penny to a widow or orphan. His enemies saw only the hard, bitter cruelty in his nature which existed there for them alone." (Good 45)

The practice of amateur psychiatry is fraught with danger (Dr. Hare advises against it), but the only way I can explain the actions of Tom Ross and Milt Good is to view Ross as a man without a conscience—and Milt Good as a decent fellow who found himself in the wrong place at the wrong time, unable to resist the power of an extremely charming and gifted psychopath.

Milt might have given a hint of this when he said, "People who know Mr. Ross know that he was a man you could not get away from easily." (Good 17) That was the tragedy of Milt Good. When he saw evil staring back at him, he should have run for his life.

Chapter Twenty: Roger Sherman

Family legend tells that before he died, Joe Sherman called his four sons into the room and made them promise not to take revenge on Dock Billingsley or his family. "No more bloodshed. We have the law. Let it do its work." The sons honored their pledge, even after Billingsley was acquitted and walked away a free man. From my perspective, eighty-seven years later, it appears that when the Shermans left the Lubbock County courthouse that afternoon in December 1917, they turned their feelings inward and were never the same after that. Theirs was a cold, unspoken fury that came from their belief that they had trusted the legal system to give them justice and it had failed them.

But Mother said they also felt anger toward Joe Sherman. He shouldn't have allowed a petty squabble to get so badly out of hand. He should have waited for the sheriff to settle the matter. He should have left his guns at home. None of the Shermans could ever bring themselves to say that Dock Billingsley deserved an acquittal, but in their secret hearts, they might have thought so. Nobody knew more about Joe Sherman's stubborn, unyielding nature than the Shermans themselves, and though they couldn't admit it, they must have understood why Dock Billingsley feared him enough to fire the first shot.

And there was guilt, the remorseless demon that stalks its victims in the middle of the night. I'm sure that Lina blamed herself. "Why didn't I stand up to him and forbid him to climb on his horse that day? Why didn't I hide his gun?" The sons roasted over the same fire. These were fine, conscientious boys and men who had been taught the frontier virtues of courage and self-reliance, and it shamed them that the man who had killed their father still walked the earth. Roger was the one most tormented by guilt—he who had been there, he who had held the rifle in his hands and could have closed the books on it forever. In 1918 he joined the army and served his tour of duty with a machinegun crew in France. After the war, he moved to New Mexico and filed on a quarter-section of land near Rencona, in the mountains southeast of Santa Fe. There he dug a well, built a cabin, and lived an isolated bachelor's life amid the pinon pines.

But he hadn't forgotten Dock Billingsley and one day in 1924 the two came face-to-face in a little general store in Rencona. Their eyes locked and Billingsley told Roger to leave. They had words, then one of them

Roger Bennett Sherman, cowboy preacher. Author's collection.

pushed the other and Billingsley fell into a shelf of canned goods. The owner of the store appeared with a shotgun and told Roger to get out. Roger left, sold two pigs at the Santa Fe market, and used the money to buy a pistol. After brooding for seven years over his missed opportunity, he had decided to finish the job. The only question was, how he would do it, as an assassination or in a fair fight?

Bad weather prevented him from carrying out his plan, first days of slow rain, and then snow. Tired of waiting, he saddled his horse and started out on the trip that would take him to Billingsley's homestead, but his horse stepped in a hole and fell, throwing Roger to the wet ground. It took him a while to catch the frightened horse, and by then Roger had taken a hard chill. He returned to his cabin and tried to warm himself in front of a roaring fire, but the chills grew worse and he was wet with perspiration. He began to realize that he had come down with pneumonia and that he was too weak to ride for help. He fell into a fevered stupor, unable to tend the fire or cook. After several days, a neighbor came to check on him but didn't enter the house when no one answered the door. For two weeks Roger lay in his sweat-soaked sheets, tormented by fever dreams about Dock Billingsley. (Roger Joe Sherman 1985: 127ff)

Mother's version of this story made Uncle Roger's bout with pneumonia a kind of epiphany. When the fever broke, he emerged with a clear vision to give his life to God and become a minister. Cousin Roger Joe Sherman's account, which I'm sure came directly from Uncle Roger, tells that the process was more gradual. In the month it took for his strength to return, Roger spent his time reading the Bible and thinking about the anger that had consumed him for so many years. When he was able to ride, he went into Rencona and began attending church services and Bible studies. As his faith grew, he came under the influence of a family friend named Ralph Hall.

Ralph Hall lived an eventful life and self-published a book about it in 1971. A competent cowboy and bronc rider, he went into the Presbyterian ministry and became a circuit-riding preacher to cow camps and small hamlets in West Texas and eastern New Mexico. Leading a packhorse with his bedroll, a change of clothes, a coffee pot, skillet, and food, he would ride from one big ranch to another, often staying out for months at a time without sleeping under a roof. When snow threatened, he kept a shovel beside his bedroll so that he could dig himself out when the storm broke. Many of the working cowboys of that day were scornful of preachers, so when Ralph showed up at a ranch, he never revealed his true profession. He went out with the cowboys, rode the outlaw horses they brought him out of the remuda, and helped with the cattle work. Having proved himself their equal in skills and work, he would offer to conduct a Christian service for them, and he was seldom refused.

In 1916 Hall drove into Seminole, Texas, to pastor its small Presbyterian church, driving a buggy pulled by two mustang horses that were so rank, he had to tie their tails together to prevent them from turning around in the traces.

"I got into Seminole late in the afternoon and drove up to the watering trough on the public square to water my team. . . . A lot of cowboys were sitting around on the green grass under the shade trees on the courthouse square." In front of the crowd, Hall's horses boogered at something, started bucking and kicking, fell down, and turned the buggy over on its side, scattering Hall and his camping gear.

"A man named Forrest Sherman was standing nearby. He piled on top of one of the horses and held him down. Two other fellows soon had Geronimo eared down," and that was Reverend Hall's introduction to the citizens of Seminole. (Ralph Hall 1971: 14-5)

Ralph and Forrest Sherman became friends, and through Forrest, the young preacher met the rest of the Sherman family. When Joe Sherman was killed the following year, Ralph Hall ministered to the family and conducted a simple graveside service. (Roger Joe Sherman 1985: 68)

In the back of the Ralph Hall book, which came into my possession after Mother's death in 1977, I found some notes she wrote on a blank page:

"Many, many times I've heard the name Ralph Hall. In fact, he must have had a tremendous influence on my Grandmother Sherman and her family. I remember so many preachings at Sawyer Flat schoolhouse, close to Loop, Texas, with dinner after church, then after a rest and lots of visiting, we would have more church in the afternoon. . . . Ralph Hall preached at these meetings." (Anna Beth Erickson notes, no date)

Ralph Hall gave strength and guidance to Uncle Roger and encouraged him to enter the ministry, and together they took their message of hope to cow camps and little towns on the fringes of America's last frontier. They founded the Ranchers Camp Meeting Movement and established branches in New Mexico (Clayton, Nogal Mesa, Magdalena), Arizona (Prescott), Wyoming (Sonoita), Colorado, Nevada (Elko), and Nebraska (Kennedy). (Roger Joe Sherman 1985: 207)

Ralph Hall remembered Uncle Roger fondly:

"We traveled from the Mexican border almost to the Canadian border; for about twenty-five years we would leave the last of May and get home about Labor Day. On thousands of nights we have unrolled our bedrolls lying side by side, out under the stars. The story of my life could also be the story of his life, for together we have lived and worked." (Ralph Hall 1971: 67)

After Uncle Roger's death in 1983, his family self-published a collection of Roger's poetry. A poem called "Journey's End" is dedicated to Ralph Hall:

"Old Pal of Mine, when day is done,
And we have each our journey run,
I hope we reach the Great Divide
And find each other side by side."
(Roger B. Sherman 1984: 1)

Chapter Twenty-one: Roy, Burt, and Olive

Roger, Forrest, and Mable were the oldest of the Sherman children and came through the ordeal of Joe Sherman's death in good shape. Roger found his calling in the ministry and raised a family in New Mexico. Mable had her home and family in Seminole, and Uncle Forrest spent his later years managing the Turkey Track ranch near Roswell, New Mexico, and had little contact with the Texas Shermans. Roy and Olive were not so lucky. They were still living at home when their father died, and, as Mother described it, "they got trapped." Something happened to Grandmother Sherman when she faced the prospect of being a widow instead of a wife. Always brave and self-reliant, she became fearful and possessive, perhaps terrified by the prospect of spending the rest of her days alone on the ranch.

Mother said that Olive was an attractive young woman. She taught herself to play the piano, enjoyed dancing, and caught the eye of several good marriage prospects, but every time a young man showed an interest in her, Grandmother found ways of running him down, using ridicule and guilt as weapons. "Aunt Olive taught Sunday school and she was very good. I can remember how happy she seemed to be when she was teaching. She always wanted to be a missionary, but that wasn't her fate." (Anna Beth Erickson notes, no date)

So Olive stayed at the ranch and the young men stopped coming around, and one day the people in Seminole began referring to her as an old maid—an old maid with a never-ending series of health problems that kept her close to her bed for the rest of her life. Uncle Roy also fell into the trap. Always the sweetest, kindest, most considerate and conscientious of the Sherman children, Roy seemed to have no defense against the force of Lina's will. With the flight of his older brothers, it fell to him to operate the ranch and take care of Olive and his mother, and Lina made sure that no scheming little hussy lured him away. When Grandmother Sherman died in 1953, Roy and Olive stayed out on the ranch, taking care of each other and sharing a fate that had left them without spouses and children. Mother said that Olive always felt bitter toward Mable, jealous that she had managed to escape and have children.

Roy and Olive lived long enough so that I knew them both, although in reflection I can see that what I knew didn't amount to much. I remember Aunt Olive as kind but shy, painfully shy. She dressed in old fashioned

From left: Roy and Lina Sherman, Mable and Buck Curry, at the Curry residence in Seminole, circa 1945. Photo courtesy Martha Marmaduke and Barbara Whitton.

clothes and wore her hair in a style that reminded me of pictures I had seen of women in the twenties, the age of the "flappers." She struck me as someone who had walked out of a museum exhibit. My conversations with her were always brief and seldom strayed beyond a few sentences of formal greeting. I could never think of anything to talk about with her. She lacked Grandmother's sense of humor and zest for life, and she seemed to have little curiosity about anything that might have interested me. She and Mother could go off into a corner and talk for hours, but I think their conversations centered on Aunt Olive's medical adventures, of which there was an unending supply.

Uncle Roy was more approachable, but within a narrow range of topics that involved the tiny world he occupied. He could always entertain me and my boy cousins with stories about the loafer wolves that once plagued cattlemen in Gaines County, and he spoke with authority about jackrabbits, coyotes, snakes, horned toads, hawks, buzzards, and storms. But that was about it. In my teenage years, I figured out that the best way to fire up a conversation with Uncle Roy was to ask, "Well, how's the grass doing?" That would loosen his tongue, but his answers far exceeded my level of interest. By the time I had developed a genuine interest in range conditions, he had become too feeble to talk.

I think the feeling we all had in the presence of Aunt Olive and Uncle Roy was sadness, a hovering sense that things had not worked out for them and that there was an emptiness in their house that could never be filled.

Uncle Burt followed a different path, although he too ended up a bachelor and spent his last days on the Sherman ranch. Born in 1897, Burt was the youngest of the boys, but he wasn't the one Grandmother wanted to hold in the nest. Short, feisty, rebellious, impatient, and maybe a bit inclined toward meanness, Burt was involved in a tragedy that seemed to haunt him the rest of his life. It was rarely mentioned in the family but I remember Mother telling me about it.

Uncle Burt was eighteen or nineteen years old, and had nagged his parents into letting him drive the family's first car, a Hupmobile. No doubt Joe and Lina lectured him about driving safely, and no doubt, in his teenage wisdom, he ignored everything they said.

One day in 1916 he was driving around in Seminole and had to stop for a little girl who was waiting on the curb to cross the street. Burt waited but she didn't step out into the street. He put the car in gear and moved forward, but then the girl changed her mind and started out into the street. Burt slammed on the brakes and waved for her to cross. She hesitated and didn't move. Burt gunned the motor and yelled for her to hurry up. When she didn't move, he lost patience, jammed the car into gear and roared away. Somehow the girl stepped in front of the car, was run over and killed.

I've never seen a shred of documentation about this incident, but I know it happened, because Aunt Bennett Kerr told my cousins the same story. Burt was not charged with a criminal offense, but it added to the other calamities that befell the Shermans—the deaths of Mary Sherman in 1916 and Joe the following year.

In 1919 Burt left the Sherman ranch and began a lifelong career as a cowboy. Here is a list of the ranches he worked:

1919-20: Cox and Heard, Seminole
1920-24: Cattle drives in Texas and New Mexico
1924-29: Ross Simpson Cedar Lake ranch, Seminole
1929-30: A. D. Jones, Tatum, New Mexico
1930-31: B. B. Curry, Seminole
1931-33: Curry and Jones, Seminole
1933-39: Fred Snyder, Whiteface
1939-41: Curry and Jones, Seminole
1941-42: Walcott ranch, Midland
1942-43: Curry and Jones, Seminole
1943-49: Higgenbotham-Dean Ranch, Lamesa
1949-51: A. C. Ward, Andrews
1951-54: L. E. Robinson, Seminole
1954-56: A. C. Ward, Andrews

In 1972 I asked Uncle Burt to write down some of his memories of cowboy life, and in a rare burst of prolixity, he sent me a six page letter, handwritten on lined notebook paper.

"The cattle business has changed so much since I worked on ranches. For one thing, the cowboys do not make the long drives we did in those days. Instead of riding ten miles to the back of the pasture to start the roundup, the boys load their horses in trailer trucks and haul them to the starting point. I do not think cowboys today are as tough as they were years ago. They do not have the hardships to go through. Many cowboys today are on the rodeo style. If I had a ranch, would never hire a man wanting to make rodeo his business. Many cowboys today never stood a night guard around a bunch of cattle with the north wind blowing snow in your face, or when the rain was falling so hard you could not see a cow only when the lightning flashed. They never had to spread their beds down on the snow-covered ground, never had to eat breakfast around a camp fire at four o'clock in the morning with snow and ice everywhere.

"Have often wished I could have been here long before my time so I could have gone on those long cattle drives the old cowboys made to Dodge City, Kansas, and other places north. The longest and the hardest drive I ever made was to White Oaks, New Mexico, northwest of Roswell. Gathered a bunch of cows off part of the Dr. Jones ranch. We went out by Tatum, New Mexico, north of Roswell, on north of Capitan Mountain, through the Black ranch. We left the Jones ranch on the twentieth of May and got back to Seminole on the fourth of July. Hope I never have to cross that old Pecos River again. It was a hard life, but carefree in a way. I have been bunged up, some horses throwing me off, falling on me, had some ribs broken, but not anything serious. Turned a pickup over once, that hurt me more than any horse ever did.

"If I was young again I would travel the same old road. There is something about the cowboy's life that gets in your blood. It was a hard life but carefree in a way. If you had a good man to work for you had it made, if you did your part. Some bosses would ask you to do things that weren't right. Never stayed with one of those." (Burt Sherman, letter 1972)

I am amazed at how fluent Uncle Burt was in this letter, considering that he spent most of his life horseback and probably wasn't a good student. But all the Shermans were literate people and readers. Aunt Bennett said that at Christmastime, they always gave each other books. (Bennett Kerr interview, 2004) They didn't write much or often, but when they did, their prose showed a high respect for the written word.

There is one part of Burt's story that puzzles me. He came into the world a rancher's son, a member of what in that time passed for landed aristocracy, yet he spent his life working for wages as a cowboy. The incongruity of this might not be apparent at once, but anyone familiar with ranching will see it as strange. In those days, and still today, rancher's sons became *ranchers*, which means they either bought or leased pasture, ran their own cattle, and hired cowboys to do the day-to-day work. Ranchers owned and managed the operation, while cowboys worked by the month and drew wages. Ranchers were tied to their land and stayed in one place, while cowboys tended to drift from job to job and ranch to ranch—as Burt most definitely did—looking for a better deal. "You may wonder why cowpunchers moved so much. More money." (Burt Sherman letter, 1972)

Old-time ranchers in Texas carried a strong sense of caste in a system that placed a high value on the acquisition of land, and to a lesser extent on money. In Burt's youth, cowboying was perceived as a kind of knighthood, but still, in leaving the caste of his birth, he must have raised eyebrows in Gaines County and caused his family some embarrassment. Uncle Burt chose to follow a carefree gypsy life, acquiring no property and taking no wife. Why? I asked him once and he gave a vague answer: "I liked being in rough country and seeing the wildlife." I suspect that he had other motives and one of them might have been rebellion against family and father. Some children seem fated to be ruled by defiance, and Burt might have been the one child out of six who drew that card.

But I think Mother had it right. She felt that Burt never escaped the memory of the child he ran over and killed, and he imposed his own sentence: to live apart from the world of people and to face the end of his days without a family of his own.

Chapter Twenty-two: Decline

In 1973 Grandmother Curry still lived in her house on Avenue E in Seminole. She was eighty-five years old and her daughters worried about her staying by herself in that big house, but any time they suggested other arrangements, they got Mable's version of the Sherman Chill. She did it well enough to put a stop to all talk about a nursing home or moving in with one of her daughters. The Curry girls didn't press the issue. Grandmother had a small legion of people who had helped her for years: Mrs. Tennill to cook, Dorothy to clean, a boy in the neighborhood to mow the yard, and handymen who trimmed the elm trees, fixed leaky faucets, and took care of routine maintenance. Once or twice a week, the Shermans (Roy, Burt, and Olive) drove into town and checked on her, and so far things were working all right. The Curry girls respected Grandmother's independent spirit and wanted her to remain in the house as long as she could.

Around the middle of April that year she fell and hurt herself, but stubborn to the end, she didn't tell anyone until the pain finally drove her to call Uncle Roy. For three days she had lived with a broken hip and the doctors had to operate and set the bone with a pin. Kris and I drove down to Seminole with my parents and visited her in the hospital. Uncle Burt had come into town from the ranch, and he and I went into the room together.

Uncle Burt was dressed in the costume he had taken up after

Mable in her rose garden near the end of her life. Photo courtesy Martha Marmaduke and Barbara Whitton.

retiring from the horseback life: khaki pants, a long-sleeved khaki shirt with the top button buttoned against the bulge of his double chin, and black cowboy boots with a tall riding heel. He had removed his straw cowboy hat and held it in work-thick fingers. In small towns in West Texas, those khaki clothes usually marked a man as a rancher, not a cowboy. Even in retirement, cowboys held tight to their blue jeans and snap-button western shirts with color and flare. The khakis were more subdued, suggesting a higher status and more of a managerial turn of mind. Uncle Roy, who wasn't present that day, always wore the same khaki uniform, and on him they seemed appropriate. On Uncle Burt, they looked good, but seemed a little out of character. They were rancher clothes, not cowboy clothes.

Grandmother was lying in a hospital bed, weak, groggy, and at times incoherent. The nurses had wrapped her right forearm in a splint to prevent her from disturbing the IV needle in her vein. I had never seen her in a bed, and the sight made me uncomfortable. It seemed very wrong that the matriarch of our family was suddenly helpless and depending on others to take care of her. Uncle Burt seemed just as uneasy as I did.

She was awake and recognized both of us, but she wasn't in her right mind. The IV needle bothered her and she seemed determined to pull it out. Uncle Burt and I exchanged glances, and he moved toward the bed and held her left hand. This seemed to irritate her, and for a moment there was a flash of anger in her blue eyes.

"Boys," she said in a creaky voice, "I want this off! Take out your knives and cut it off." We didn't know what to say. "All right, if you won't do what I ask, I'll do it myself!"

We called for a nurse who came and gave Grandmother a gentle scolding. As soon as the nurse left, Grandmother went back to work on the splint, but her fingers lacked the strength to do the job. A young doctor breezed into the room, glanced at her chart, and talked to her. I was astonished when he called her "Mable." MABLE! This young upstart, fresh out of medical school, had no idea what he was saying. *This was Mrs. Curry*! He wanted another X-ray of the hip, and soon a male technician entered, and as casually as if he were uncovering a side of beef, pulled back the covers and slipped an X-ray plate beneath Grandmother's hip.

The Curry home in winter. Photo courtesy Martha Marmaduke and Barbara Whitton.

That was too much for me and Uncle Burt. Mortal eyes were not meant to see Mrs. Curry in a hospital gown. We left. Grandmother closed her eyes and took the indignities without a murmur.

In the waiting room, I heard Mother and Aunt Bennett talking about Grandmother's confused state of mind. One night she had told Aunt Bennett that she had given birth to twins, and she spoke of having a baby beside her bed. Another time, she awoke with a smile and said, "Your father would have thought that was funny." But most of the time, she talked of going home. She begged her daughters to take her home. In lucid moments, she kept her sense of humor and joked with my father, whom she had always liked. When Joe Erickson asked how she was feeling, she gave him a piercing blue gaze and said, "Rotten, thank you." When Joe left the room, he said, "Don't speak to any strange men while we're gone." Grandmother smiled and said, "I certainly won't."

She died four months later in Roswell, New Mexico, where she had been moved to be close to my Aunt Drucilla. Joe Erickson called me at seven o'clock on the morning of August 22, 1973, and said she had died in her sleep the night before.

Curry sisters as young ladies. From left: Bennett, Drucilla, Anna Beth, Jonye, and Mary. Photo courtesy Martha Marmaduke and Barbara Whitton.

Chapter Twenty-three: Grandmother's Funeral

Kris and I drove down to Seminole the next day and joined some of the family at Grandmother's house. Around six, we went to the funeral home and viewed the body. The gray metal casket had been placed in a small room, and I stayed for half an hour or more. I had not yet gotten a feeling of death about Grandmother. I looked into her face and marveled. After she had lived eighty-five years on the Llano Estacado, braving wind and blizzards and sand storms, her face showed hardly a wrinkle and was still as smooth and white as alabaster. This was no trick of the undertaker's trade. Mrs. Curry had preserved her beauty through constant care . . . and some quality of the spirit that I don't claim to understand. Only her hands showed the wear of years, and the undertaker had covered them with satin. I moved the fabric and looked at them. They reminded me of the gnarled shapes of cottonwood trees that have been sculpted by wind and storm. I touched her hands and face, and left the room, knowing that she was no longer with us.

By the time we returned to the house, all the immediate family had arrived: the Pattersons from Houston; the Harters from Amarillo and Lubbock; the Cieszinskis from Roswell, Santa Fe, and Lubbock; and the Ericksons from Perryton and Amarillo. Aunt Mary Curry was there too, she the only Curry girl who had never married. She had driven from California where for some years she had belonged to a religious cult run by a woman named Clair Prophet. My father said that when Aunt Mary arrived in Seminole, she had to borrow a few dollars to buy gas for her car. She had several gold bars hidden in her luggage, each worth about thirty thousand dollars, but no cash. I had never gotten close to Aunt Mary, and I doubt that many people had, even her sisters. Aunt Bennett said that in her youth, Mary rode the wildest horses and drove the fastest cars, and before she left Seminole, she had dusted up a scandal or two. She seemed to have inherited all the eccentricities from both sides of the family and then added a few of her own.

That night, the grandchildren spent the night at Grandmother's house, while the aunts and uncles found quieter lodgings at the Raymond Motel. After brushing my teeth in the bathroom, I noticed a little note in Grandmother's handwriting taped to the tank of the commode: "Please watch after you flush. Sometimes it hangs. The water will run until you shake the handle." I had to laugh. Mrs. Curry had not quite given up her hold on the house she had occupied for sixty-two years.

Around nine the next morning, the Sherman contingent from Roswell arrived for the funeral: Sam and Edward B. Sherman, the sons of Uncle Forrest and Aunt Mary D, and their wives, as well as Uncle Roger and Aunt Bessie. They were almost strangers to me and I wasn't sure why. Mother had said, "They're very Sherman," which I took to mean that they kept to themselves and steered a course around family entanglements. There may have also been some lingering bitterness about Joe Sherman's opposition to Uncle Forrest's marriage to Mary D Ramsey—good heavens, more than fifty years ago.

I introduced myself to Uncle Roger and Aunt Bessie, although they knew who I was: Anna Beth's boy. Uncle Roger wore a dark suit and tie and carried his eighty-one years with dignity. Aunt Bessie must have been a few years younger than Uncle Roger, and was as cute as a button. Dressed in the traditional black funeral dress, she had sparkling dark eyes that missed nothing, and she greeted all the nieces and nephews with a smile and kind words. I wished that I could steer Uncle Roger off into a quiet corner so that I might ask him some questions about his father, but the opportunity never presented itself. And I doubt that he would have said much anyway.

At nine-thirty we loaded into cars and drove to the South Seminole Baptist Church, where Grandmother taught a Sunday school class for many years. By then, we had gotten a news flash from the Sherman ranch: Roy and Olive weren't feeling well and would not attend the funeral, and nobody knew about Uncle Burt. He hadn't shown up.

Black is the color we usually associate with funerals, but in Seminole the predominant color seemed to be yellow. The grass in the vacant lot across from Grandmother's house had turned August yellow, the hearse and limousine were yellow, and so was the brick on the church, the austere yellow that seems to have some odd appeal to Baptists in West Texas. Inside the church, we saw more yellow in the pews and woodwork. It wasn't a particularly pleasant color, but maybe appropriate for the drought-prone Llano Estacado.

On the church steps, we formed up in lines: Curry daughters and their husbands first, followed by Uncle Roger and Aunt Bessie, Sam and Edward B., then the grandchildren. As we filed into the church, I glanced backward and noticed the license plate on the yellow hearse: "AWE 849."

The inside of the church was plain and simple, almost stark, the walls white and adorned only with fluorescent light fixtures and plastic "stained glass" windows. The ceiling consisted of squares of fiberboard, some browned by water leaks. The baptistery at the front showed a large picture of a river flowing from a range of snow-capped mountains in the background. It didn't much resemble the country Jesus walked or the Llano Estacado.

The church was only about one-quarter filled, less an indication of Grandmother's prestige in the town than the fact that she had outlived most of her friends. The family filled three rows at the front, twenty-seven of us in all. The minister, a short stocky man with dark eyes and a balding head, read from the Gospel of John, which he said was one of Grandmother's favorite passages, and a duet rendered a creaky version of "How Great Thou Art." Then the minister delivered a short sermon on heaven. Funeral services seldom do justice to the deceased, and this one proved no exception. I doubt that the preacher knew Mrs. Curry very well and his service gave no hint that we had gathered to say goodbye to a woman I had always regarded as truly extraordinary.

He might have mentioned that she was born in the first town to appear on the Llano Estacado, at a time when wild mustangs still galloped across an unfenced sea of prairie grass, and lived to see Braniff jets making their daily run from Midland to Dallas. He could have mentioned that she studied Shakespeare and Latin with nuns in a convent, matched wills against an overbearing father, and shepherded five daughters through the Great Depression.

He might have mentioned her lifelong struggle against the entropic forces of West Texas; her pride, beauty, and intelligence; that she and her husband had left behind the largest private library in Gaines County; that in spite of the corrosive effects of climate and disease and family strife, she remained loving, dignified and strong to the very end. He might have quoted this moving tribute to all Texas women, written by Celia Morris, the one-time wife of noted editor and author, Willie Morris:

> "[The] typical Texas woman brought up children and kept families together. She raised and cooked their food; made and maintained their clothes; worked to make their shelters life-enhancing. She planted fruits and flowers and created much of what grace there has been in daily life. She moved from the farms and prairies and then to towns and to cities, weaving the fabric of community as she went.
>
> "She taught in schools and tended the sick. She filled the churches, which have been the major institutional force in this state that has worked to make a gentler ethic prevail. She helped others live and helped them die." (Celia Morris in Clifford and Pilkington 1989: 112)

Or he might have set aside his sermon and turned to the two rows of grandchildren and said something simple. "You were very lucky to have known this woman. When you're looking around for a model of what it is to be a woman, a lady, a mother, a human being, remember Mrs. B. B. Curry." There were many things he might have said, had he known her well, but he didn't. Preachers move in and out of a community, and they have to bury strangers with words they don't feel. So Mrs. Curry was sent on her last journey in a drab little church, without poetry or grand music or even a sentence that might have told us who she was.

After the service, we loaded up in our cars and started the slow procession to the cemetery. At every intersection, a police car blocked traffic and a policeman stood at attention as we passed. On Main Street, cars pulled over to the side and let us pass. These are common gestures of respect in small towns, and I appreciated them. We drove south out of town until we reached the cemetery on the edge of Seminole Draw, the same dry streambed that cut through Buck Curry's ranch some twenty miles northwest of town. As we approached the canopy over the gravesite, the pallbearers were coming up with the casket, struggling past tombstones and directed by a funeral home employee in blue overalls. As they approached the device on which the casket was to be placed, one of the pallbearers gasped, "You don't reckon we'll fall into the hole, do you?"

Grandmother was laid to rest beside Buck Curry's grave and just a short distance from the Sherman family plot. Joe and Lina Sherman rested there, beside the grave of their little girl, Mary. Near the Sherman plot stood a sign that read, "Posted No Guns." I smiled at that, wondering if Old Joe Sherman had been floating around at night, looking for Dock Billingsley. When the casket had been set in place, the immediate family moved under the canopy and took the chairs in front of the grave. Suddenly Uncle Burt appeared, wearing his funeral suit, cowboy boots, watch fob, and straw hat, and took his place with the family. In a grumpy voice, much too loud for the setting, he told Aunt Bennett, "Well, nobody told me what time the funeral started!"

Uncle Burt and Barbara Harter Whitton mugging for the cameras. Kris Erickson in the background between them. Photo courtesy of Barbara Whitton.

The graveside service was brief and the crowd broke up into small knots. Then we all drove back to Grandmother's house, which was now packed with friends and family. At eleven, we lined up and filled our paper plates with the food that had been brought by the ladies of the church: fresh blackeyed peas, okra, green beans, squash, roast beef, meat loaf, fried chicken, jello salads, and enough pies, cakes, and cobblers to founder an army.

After the meal, we went out to the front lawn for photographs. Here, Uncle Burt was the darling of all the nieces and grand-nieces. They hugged his neck and kissed him on the cheek while the shutters clicked. Wearing his cowboy hat and puffing on a cigar, the old bachelor loved the attention but pretended not to. The photographer tried to coax a smile out of him.

"I don't want to smile."

"Say cheese!"

"I don't like cheese." The pictures will show that he finally gave up and smiled.

Before long, Uncle Burt said that he had to be getting back to the ranch, which caused me and my cousins to laugh. Over the years, that had become the signature line of Uncles Roy and Burt: "Well, I need to be getting back to the ranch." It struck us as funny because those two old bachelors and their old-maid sister lived such a quiet, uncluttered existence that there was never a reason for them to rush back to the ranch.

What did they have to do? Uncle Roy gathered the eggs, Aunt Olive fed the chickens, and Uncle Burt fed his cat and the wild cottontail rabbits that he had turned into pets. After that, "the boys," as everyone in the family called Roy and Burt, would read a book or *The Cattleman* magazine, while Aunt Olive did some needlework. At six o'clock sharp, they would eat a bite of supper and retire to their rooms. There was nothing at the ranch that demanded their attention, but they could tolerate crowds and kinfolks and the noise of town only in small doses, and then they had to scurry back to the country. They were "very Sherman." Uncle Burt left, muttering, "I've never had so many women hanging on my neck or seen so many cameras in my whole life!"

In the afternoon, some of my male cousins and I decided to drive out to the Curry ranch, hoping we might find something left of the old ranch house where Buck used to stay during the summer months. There, comfortable in his bastion of male squalor, he was able to escape the noise and strain of a house that contained six women. Until winter drove him back to town, he could read his books, build his spurs, and pet his dogs. Cousin Jim Harter led us to the spot, northwest of town, and we were disappointed to find that nothing remained of the house, or anything else that resembled a ranch. Sometime in the fifties, Grandmother had leased out the eight thousand acres to a farmer named Fred Barrett, who had bulldozed the mesquite and shinnery, plowed the sod, drilled irrigation wells, and planted it all to cotton, potatoes, and peaches.

For better or worse, the farmers had won Gaines County and the ranching community had vanished like a flash of lightning in the night sky. By 1973 almost every square inch of the county had come under the plow, and one of the few patches of native vegetation lay on the Sherman ranch east of town. That piece of ground would never feel the scrape of a plow as long as the Shermans were still alive.

We walked down to Seminole Draw and began to notice the oppressive heat. The temperature was 105 that afternoon, and every living thing wilted under the glare of the sun. It reminded me of what a hard and stingy country this was, and though the Shermans and Buck Curry had claimed to love it, I couldn't help feeling some relief that I would probably never inherit any of Buck's land. With five daughters as heirs, and nobody in the family inclined toward farming, the land would be sold. I had always felt nostalgic about the Curry land, but after seeing it in the middle of August, I left with fewer illusions than I'd had before I got there.

Back at the house in Seminole, we found the five Curry girls sitting at the dining table, discussing in somber tones the task they had all been dreading, dividing up Grandmother's possessions and clearing out the house. They had dreaded it because of its awful finality. This house, where we had gathered so many times for weddings and funerals and family reunions, had held us together for as long as any of us could remember. It had been a place that never changed. Since 1911 it had held the unmistakable stamp of Mable Curry's will, and it seemed almost unthinkable that, within a few weeks' time, it would be stripped bare, put on the market for sale, and occupied by strangers.

But it had to be done, and done quickly, so the sisters devised a lottery system for dividing up the silver, china, and furniture, and sent the grandchildren into the library to divide up the books. This would be a formidable task, disposing of a library that covered three entire walls. The Harter brothers and I had to make a quick trip to Hobbs, New Mexico, to gather a supply of sturdy liquor boxes from trash receptacles. (Seminole was in a dry county and offered an inferior grade of cardboard boxes, those intended for lettuce, grapefruit, and canned soup).

That night, the grandchildren gathered in the library and made the division, keeping all the various collections intact: Civil War, Founding Fathers, New Mexico History, Texana, and so forth. My cousins were generous enough to give me the entire Texana collection, recognizing that I had aspirations of one day becoming a Texas author and would put the collection to good use. This I have done, dear cousins. At some point in this exercise, Mike Harter commented on the irony of thirteen grandchildren, all with high school diplomas and some with college degrees, doing hard labor to disperse a library accumulated by a man with four grades of formal schooling.

West Texas was settled by people who found their own way to books and fashioned their own education out of the materials at hand. In the towns they erected on the prairie, they left behind twelve-grade schools made of brick and mortar. I would like to believe that those of us who attended those schools are better and smarter than the ones who built them, but I doubt that we are.

The next morning, we all said our goodbyes and went our separate ways. Before leaving, I went back into the house and took one last look around. It seemed terribly empty and barren now. There was Grandmother's wheelchair in the hall and her empty chair at the dining table, and a great void that had once been filled with her presence. She wasn't there any more. The place had become just another house.

Chapter Twenty-four: And Then There Was One

After Grandmother Curry's death, Olive, Burt, and Roy continued living out at the Sherman ranch in a ready-built house they had moved in from Lubbock sometime in the 1950s. It was more modern and convenient than the old house, with inside plumbing, electricity, and gas heat, and located closer to the blacktop highway. Uncle Roy tore down the original ranch house. (Mike Harter letter, December 29, 2004).

Olive and Roy Sherman as children. Photo courtesy Martha Marmaduke and Barbara Whitton.

Of the three surviving Shermans, Burt enjoyed the best health and took over all the housework, cooking and cleaning and taking care of Olive. She had been sickly all her adult life and that pattern continued. Occasional letters from Uncle Roy said that Olive was in and out of her sickbed, in and out of the hospital, first brought down by some malady and then miraculously cured. In 1978 Roy's health began to fail. He had severe arthritis in his hands and knees, and in the summer of 1979 he had a bad spell with his heart and had to spend a week in the Seminole hospital. One evening after Roy came back home, Uncle Burt dropped dead on the kitchen floor. Olive found him.

So once again the clan gathered in Seminole for another funeral. I was not able to attend, as I had just taken a cowboy job on the Beaver River in Oklahoma, but I heard about it from my father. My aunts and Sam Sherman went to Seminole thinking that they would need to put Olive and Roy in a rest home, or make some kind of arrangements to care for them. Roy was so crippled he could hardly walk, but when Sam offered to gather the eggs, Roy said no thank you. A stranger would upset the hens and then they wouldn't lay. So Roy hobbled outside to his pickup, drove a hundred feet to the hen house, and gathered the eggs himself. Later, Sam found a snake in the yard. He went for a garden hoe, but when he returned, the snake was gone. When he told Roy about it, Roy said, "Yes, that's our bullsnake. He catches mice under the house."

Aunt Olive worried about Burt's cat. Burt was the only one who had ever fed her. When Sam tried to feed the cat, she took one look at him and disappeared. Aunt Olive sighed, "She's not used to strangers."

Aunt Drucilla tried to persuade Roy and Olive to move to Roswell, where she could look after them. No. So Aunt Dru hired a woman in Seminole to drive out to the ranch every day and cook for them. That didn't last long. The Shermans had always eaten a big breakfast at seven o'clock sharp, and they couldn't start the day without steak, fresh eggs, biscuits and gravy. The woman made the long early morning drive out to the ranch for two days and quit. That was fine with Roy and Olive, and as pleasantly as they could, they invited Sam Sherman,

Olive's needlepoint pillow, showing a hair style similar to the one she wore most of her life. Photo courtesy of Kris Erickson.

Aunt Drucilla, Aunt Jonye, and Aunt Bennett to go back home. They would be all right.

One month after Burt's death, Uncle Roy died in his sleep, on the same day Grandmother Curry had died six years before in 1973. Sam Sherman hired a man to round up and sell the few remaining Sherman cattle, and Aunt Olive finally decided to leave the ranch and move to a rest home—a lifelong invalid who had outlived all of her brothers and sisters. One of my aunts went out to the ranch to pack up some clothes for Aunt Olive, and had to enter Aunt Olive's room, a place where she had never been before. What she saw caused her to stare in amazement. The room was filled with dolls.

Chapter Twenty-five: Afterthoughts

Dan Flores had a low opinion of West Texas memoirs and dismissed most of them as "naive horse operas that resonate nineteenth-century ancestor worship rather than twentieth- and twenty-first century significance." (Flores 1990: 165) I have not intended this to be a naive horse opera. I view it as the story of a group of people who were never as virtuous or strong or knowledgeable as they wished to be, but who managed to dignify their times and places in spite of their shortcomings. They didn't give much thought to "twentieth- and twenty-first century significance," or if they did, it never occurred to them to write about it. Until I came along, nobody in my family had ever dreamed that someone from Seminole or Perryton could aspire to being a writer, or that life in rural Texas would be worth recording. They were so busy raising children, washing clothes, plucking chickens, and battling the elements of nature, the instinct to pause, observe, and record the details of their lives never had a chance to take root.

They were modest people who tried to avoid anything that smacked of self-promotion or self-absorption. They kept no diaries, burned most of their letters, and shunned the recorders of local and regional history. They seemed content to be remembered through their deeds and their children. Most of those children also burned their letters, but some, especially my mother, passed along a rich heritage through the telling of stories.

One member of my family who was inclined to take a broader view of things, and wrote down her thoughts, was a Sherman-by-marriage, Aunt Mary D, the wife of Forrest Sherman—a woman I never knew but wish I had. I doubt that she would have placed a high value on the little manuscript she wrote for her grandchildren, but I have found it wise and illuminating. In writing about her own family, the Ramseys, and her husband's people, the Shermans, she dealt with the questions: Who are we and what have we done on this earth?

"The great outdoors does something for people. The prairie and sky had a way of trimming people down to size or changing them into giants—into people to whom nothing seemed impossible. They came to a big country needing big men and women to live in it. There was no place for the weak, man or woman. We were brought up to know that the cow people were good people, with stamina, courage, and a capacity for endurance. Many of the men were rough in their speech and given to vigorous action, and they were let alone and respected, but close association revealed much kindness about the inner man.

"My people were strong, independent, and adventurous. They lived close to nature and God. We read at night by lamplight from the few books we had. We were taught not to substitute education for intelligence. My parents spoke on matters of principle always. This is a little sketch of your cowboy ancestors. I think you should learn something about them. You have a little of their blood in you—and it is good blood." (Mary D Sherman manuscript, no date: 6-7)

It seems strange now that after all their scuffling on the Llano Estacado, the Shermans, Underhills, and Currys left no seeds to sprout on the land they so desperately wanted. The only members of my family left in Gaines County are in the cemetery. The Curry girls married men who had no desire to shoot dice against the weather, and moved on to Houston, Roswell, Lubbock, and Perryton. Both of the family ranches, seventeen thousand acres that gave misery and meaning to the Currys and Shermans, have passed into other hands, probably the great-grandchildren of "nesters." In good years, that red sandy soil fulfills every dream that floated through the mind of Paris Cox. In bad years, it confirms the darkest expectations of the early explorers.

For those of us who carry the blood of West Texas pioneers into the twenty-first century, what remains is a memory—insubstantial, yes, but also possessing a reality that defies the erosion of wind and time. Buildings rise and fall, land changes hands, fashions come and go, and money is only paper backed by promises. What endures is a memory projected upon the mind in the form of stories, a fully recollected past that will guide us into a future of unknown possibilities and dangers.

I hope we and our children are able to respond with some of the courage, strength, intelligence, and vigor displayed by our forebears. If we remember them well, maybe we shall.

Author with Aunt Bennett Kerr, 2004. Photo by Kris Erickson.

References

Books

Boller, Paul F. Jr. 1992. *Memoirs of an Obscure Professor*. Fort Worth: Texas Christian University Press.

Bronwell, Nancy. 1980. *Lubbock: A Pictorial History*. Virginia Beach, VA: The Donning Company.

Clifford, Craig, and Pilkington, Tom, eds. 1989. *Range Wars: Heated Debates, Sober Reflections, and Other Assessments of Texas Writing*. Dallas: Southern Methodist University Press.

Coleman, Max M. 1952. *From Mustanger to Lawyer*. Lubbock: Privately published.

Curry, W. Hubert. 1979. *Sun Rising on the West: The Saga of Henry Clay and Elizabeth Smith*. Crosbyton, TX: Crosby County Pioneer Memorial Museum.

Dixon, Olive King. 1927. *The Life of Billy Dixon: Plainsman, Scout, and Pioneer*. Revised edition. Dallas: The Southwest Press.

Eidson, Fay and Hull, Pat W. nd. *Martin County, The First Thirty Years*. Seagraves, TX: Pioneer Book Publishers.

Elliot, W. J. 1939. *The Spurs*. Spur, TX: The Texas Spur, Publishers.

Emmett, Chris. 1953. *Shanghai Pierce: A Fair Likeness*. Norman: University of Oklahoma Press.

Erickson, John R. 1995. *Through Time and the Valley*. Denton: University of North Texas Press.

_____. 1994. *Catch Rope: Long Arm of the Cowboy*. Denton: University of North Texas Press.

Exley, Jo Ella Powell. 2001. *Frontier Blood: The Saga of the Parker Family*. College Station: Texas A&M University Press.

Fulmore, Z. T. 1915. *History and Geography of Texas as Told in County Names*. Austin: E. L. Steck, Publishers.

Gaines County Historical Survey Committee. 1974. *The Gaines County Story: A History of Gaines County, Texas*. Seagraves, TX: Pioneer Book Publishers.

Garza County Historical Survey Committee. 1980. *Wagon Wheels: A History of Garza County*. Burnet, TX: Eakin Publications.

Good, Milt, as told to W. E. Lockhart. 1935. *Twelve Years in a Texas Prison*. Amarillo, TX: Russell Stationery Company.

Graves, John. 1960. *Goodbye To A River*. New York: Alfred Knopf.

Graves, Lawrence L., ed. 1962. *A History of Lubbock*. Lubbock: West Texas Museum Association.

Hall, Ralph. 1971. *The Main Trail*. San Antonio: The Naylor Company.

Haley, J. Evetts. 1936. *Charles Goodnight, Cowman and Plainsman*. Boston: Houghton Mifflin Company.

_____. 1967. *The XIT Ranch of Texas and the Early Days of the Llano Estacado*. Norman: University of Oklahoma Press.

Hare, Robert D., Ph.D. 1993. *Without Conscience: The Disturbing World of the Psychopaths Among Us*. New York: Guilford Press.

Hill, Frank P., and Jacobs, Pat Hill. 1986. *Grassroots Upside Down: A History of Lynn County, Texas*. Austin: Nortex Press.

Holden, William Curry. 1934. *The Spur Ranch*. Boston: The Christopher Publishing House.

_____1932. *Rollie Burns: An Account of the Ranching Industry on the South Plains*. Dallas: The Southwest Press.

_____. 1970. *The Espuela 1970 Land and Cattle Company: A Study of a Foreign-Owned Ranch in Texas*. Austin: Texas State Historical Association.

Huckabay, Ida Lasater. 1949. *Ninety-four Years in Jack County*, 1854-1948. Waco: Texian Press.

Hunt, George M. 1919. *Early Days Upon the Plains of Texas*. Lubbock: Privately published.

Hunter, J. Marvin, ed. and Saunders, George W., director. 1925. *The Trail Drivers of Texas*. Nashville: Cokesbury Press.

Jackson, Grace. 1959. *Cynthia Ann Parker*. San Antonio: The Naylor Company.

Jenkins, John Cooper, et. al. 1986. *Estacado: Cradle of Culture and Civilization On the Staked Plains of Texas*. Crosbyton, TX: Crosby County Pioneer Memorial Museum.

McNeill III, J.C. "Cap". 1988. *The McNeills' SR Ranch*. College Station: Texas A&M University Press.

Murrah, David J. 1981. *C.C. Slaughter: Rancher, Banker, Baptist*. Austin: University of Texas Press.

Palo Pinto Historical Commission, 1986. *History of Palo Pinto County Texas*. Dallas: Curtis Media Corporation.

Post, Texas, Chamber of Commerce, Women's Division. 1988. *Foot Prints: A History of Garza County and Its People*. Dallas: Taylor Publishing Company.

Rathjen, Frederick W. 1998. *The Texas Panhandle Frontier*. Lubbock: Texas Tech University Press.

Sherman, Roger Bennett. 1984. *Mountain Solitude: A Collection of Poems by Roger Bennett Sherman*. Privately printed.

Sherman, Roger Joe. 1985. *Pastor of the Range: A Biography of a Southwest Missionary*. Pompano Beach, FL: Exposition Press.

Smithson, Fay Eidson, and Hull, Pat Wilkinson. 1970. *Martin County: The First Thirty Years*. Hereford, TX: Pioneer Book Publishers, Inc.

Spikes, Nellie Witt and Ellis, Temple Ann. 1952. *Through the Years: A History of Crosby County, Texas*. San Antonio: The Naylor Company.

Yoakum, H., 1935. *History of Texas*, volume 2. Austin: The Steck Company, Austin. Facsimile reproduction of the original published in 1855.

Von-Maszewski, W. M. and Von-Maszewski, Matthew E. 1983. *Index to the Trail Drivers of Texas*. Houston: Tortuga Press.

Wallace, Ernest, and Hoebel, E. Adamson. 1952. *The Comanches, Lords of the South Plains*. Norman: University of Oklahoma Press.

Wilbarger, J. W. 1953. *Indian Depredations in Texas*. Austin: The Steck Company. Facsimile reproduction of the original published in 1889.

References

Magazine Articles and Pamphlets

Clarke, Mary Whatley. 1971. Bad Man . . . Good Man? *The Cattleman*, December, 43, 62.

Coleman, Max M. 1931. Law and Order. *Frontier Times,* December, 141-2.

Hall, Claude. 1947. The Early History of Floyd County. *Panhandle Plains Historical Review.*

The Historic Carmelite Monastery and Our Lady of Mercy Academy. nd. The Martin County Convent, Inc., Stanton, Texas.

Marshall, Doyle. 1985. Red Haired 'Indian' Raiders on the Texas Frontier. *West Texas Historical Association Year Book*, volume 61, 88-89, 97.

Panorama of the Past. 1956. Pamphlet. No author listed. Weatherford.

Interviews and Unpublished Manuscripts

Erickson, Anna Beth Curry. 1972. "Memories of Tom Ross." Unpublished manuscript in the possession of the author.

_____. Interview June 15, 1970.

_____. Interview July 21, 1976.

_____. Notes written in the back of Ralph Hall's book. No date.

Gracy, Mrs. Alice. nd. "Willis Day Twichell" Unpublished manuscript in the archives of Panhandle Plains Historical Museum, Canyon.

Haydon, Mrs. Charles. 1925. Unpublished manuscript, copied from microfilm by Edith Standhardt in 1965.

_____. 1965. Unpublished manuscript based on an interview with Edith Stanhardt, May 27, 1965.

Kerr, Bennett Harter. Interview with the author September 2, 1972.

_____. Interview with the author August 7, 2004.

_____. Interview with Jim Harter. December 25, 2004.

Quillen, Jane Lowe. nd. "Old Quaker Colony." Unpublished manuscript in the archives of the Panhandle-Plains Historical Museum, Canyon, Texas.

Sherman, Burt. Interview with the author. December 1969.

References

Sherman, Mary D Ramsey. nd. Untitled manuscript written for her
    grandchildren.
Sherman, Roy. Interview with Edith Standhardt. Seminole, Texas. 1963.
    _____ Interview with the author, September 14, 1971.
Singer, Charles. Taped interview, Rogers, Arkansas, June 1981.
    Southwest Collection, Lubbock.

Newspapers

Alley, John P., as told to Frank Hill. "Fifty-four Years of Pioneering on
    the South Plains," a series of thirteen articles appearing in the
    Lubbock Daily Journal. 1932. Southwest Collection, Lubbock.
Bean, Tom and Hawley, Scrub. "Rustler Tom Ross Died Young, But
    Still Years Past His Time." *Livestock Weekly*, May 2, 1996. (This
    article draws heavily from a master's thesis, "Tom Ross: Outlaw
    and Stockman," written at the University of Texas-El Paso in 1979
    by James I. Fenton).
Clarksville Standard, Clarksville, Texas. December 22, 1860.
Crosbyton Review, July 22, 1917. Story of Joe Sherman's death.
Dallas Herald. January 2, 1861. Letter from Sul Ross.
Fairley, Bill. "Making It Hot For Rustlers." *Fort Worth Star-Telegram*,
    Fort Worth, Texas. June 23, 1999.
Lubbock Avalanche-Journal. September 1, 1959. Interview with George
    Singer's Daughter. George W. Singer file, Southwest Collection.
    Lubbock.
Seminole Sentinel: Joe Sherman's death: June 7, 1917; October 18, 1917;
    November 29, 1917. Tom Ross: November 23, 1922; December
    12, 1922; April 26, 1923.

Letters

Clinesmith, Sarrah. Letter to Joe Sherman. July 13, 1902.
    _____. Letter to Joe Sherman. May 24, 1891.
Coleman, Max. Letter to Seymour Conner, no date. George W. Singer
    file, Southwest Collection, Lubbock, Texas.

Curry, Mable Sherman. Letter to the author. October 21, 1969.

_____. Letter to the author. January 15, 1972.

Graves, John. Letter to the author. March 30, 1974.

_____. Letter to the author. September 14, 1974.

_____. Letter to the author, November 8, 1978.

_____. Letter to the author, August 7, 1979.

Haley, J. Evetts. Letter to the author. February 17, 1977.

_____. Letter to the author. April 13, 1978

Harter, J. Michael, letter to the author. June, 1998

_____, letter to the author. July 13, 2004.

_____. Letter to the author. July 17, 2004.

_____. Letter to the author. December 29, 2004.

Sherman, Burt. Letter to the author. November 22, 1972.

Sherman, Joe. Letter to Josie Hawkins, April 9, 1887.

Sherman, Roy. Letter to the author. September 27, 1969.

_____. Letter to the author, October 22, 1969.

_____. Letter to the author, February 3, 1970.

Index

Index

Index